Six Plays

Six Plays

by
SLAWOMIR MROZEK

translated by
NICHOLAS BETHELL

GROVE PRESS, INC.
NEW YORK

Library of Congress Catalog Card Number: 67-24103
Fifth Printing

DISTRIBUTED BY RANDOM HOUSE, INC., NEW YORK

Manufactured in the United States of America

GROVE PRESS, INC., 53 EAST 11TH STREET,
NEW YORK, NEW YORK 10003

Contents

The Police

Translated from the Polish *Policja*

Author's note on the production of The Police

This play does not contain anything except what it actually contains. This means that it is not an allusion to anything, it is not a metaphor, and it should not be read as such. The most important thing is to present the naked text, as exactly as possible, with a firmly underlined sense of logic in the opinions and scenes. The play, provided it is in fact staged, will demand intense concentration on the part of the audience because of its structural compactness. So unless the production is clear and pure, the play will be a tiring one.

The statement that this play is not a metaphor, but is simply what it is (within its own area and time of duration), entails the following consequences:

No scenographic tricks must be added to the play, either for the sake of humour or for the sake of decoration (decorativeness). Nothing need be 'emphasized', and 'atmosphere' should be treated with great care. No over-contrived action should be added to the play. In a word, nothing should be done to detract from the transparency of the production, which must be stern and static, clean and 'snake in the grass'-like. Bitter experience shows that any attempt at exaggerated 'emphasizing', 'interpreting' or overacting this author's texts will be an artistic failure.

Nor is the play (God forbid) a comedy, which means that the jokes in it must not be over-accentuated. Whatever jokes the play may contain, they are not the sort of jokes to be told in a voice which implies, 'Pay attention! I am about to tell you a joke.' If my advice is ignored, the result will be a failure. It will be inelegant, if not tasteless.

Neither is this a 'modern' or an 'experimental' play. It is certainly neither of these. I do not think I need expand on this.

I imagine that what I have just written will lay me open to the charge that I do not understand theatricality. This is not the point. Perhaps I do not understand theatricality. Perhaps I do not even feel it. But one thing I do know, and that is that certain elements of so-called 'theatricality' and of theatrical thought have become entirely banal. They have made themselves shallow and a fetish, and have entered somehow into the arsenal of a thought which is thoughtless and automatic. Apart from anything else the reading of plays as metaphors, which is capable of being creative and new, is also capable of being transformed into yet another pattern of thought. (All the more so since the little play in question can provoke one to 'make life easier' by applying such labels as 'metaphor', 'comedy', 'modern' and suchlike.)

While I know what this little play is not, I do not know what it is, and it is not my duty to explain what it is. This must be discovered by the theatre. And if anyone imagines that these author's remarks and 'nots' limit the producer or leave him without a job to do, it means that the person has no true respect for the theatre. The theatre is not so cramped and poverty-stricken as he thinks.

THE AUTHOR

Characters

The Chief of Police

The Prisoner
*A former revolutionary, later the general's
aide-de-camp*

The Police Sergeant
An agent-provocateur

The Wife of the Sergeant-Provocateur

The General

A Policeman

*Acts I and III take place in the Chief of
Police's office.
Act II takes place in the house of the
Sergeant-Provocateur*

Act One

In the CHIEF OF POLICE'*s office, which has a desk, two chairs and all other essential props. The office door is in a prominent position and there are two pictures on the wall. One is of the Infant King (a baby in an old-fashioned pram or a child dressed in the style of the nineteenth-century bourgeoisie), and the other of the Regent (a frightening-looking old man with a moustache). All those in any way connected with the police have big moustaches. The* PRISONER-REVOLUTIONARY *has a pointed beard like those of nineteenth-century progressives. All the policemen have jackboots, swords and high stiff collars. The interrogator has a civilian jacket, short and close fitting. The uniforms, which are all navy blue, have very shiny metal buttons.*

CHIEF OF POLICE (*standing up and reading the end of some document*). ... and so with feelings of shame and disgust I renounce my crimes, and the only desire I have is to serve our government with all my strength and with the deepest veneration and love for the rest of my life. (*Sits down, folds up the document.*)

PRISONER. Don't put it away. I'll sign it.

CHIEF. You'll sign it! What?

PRISONER. I'll sign it and that's that.

CHIEF. But why?

PRISONER. What do you mean, why? For ten years you examine me, interrogate me, keep me in prison. Every day for ten years you give me that form to sign. When I refuse you threaten me with dreadful punishments and try to talk me round. Finally I agree to sign so that I can get out of prison and serve the government, and you look surprised and ask me why.

CHIEF. But it's so sudden, and without warning.

PRISONER. Colonel, I am undergoing a drastic change.

CHIEF. What change?

PRISONER. A drastic change of heart. I don't want to fight the government any more.

CHIEF. Why not?

PRISONER. I'm fed up with it. If anyone wants to fight the government, let them. I don't know who's going to do it. Spies for a foreign power, perhaps? Secret agents? But not me any more. I've done my bit.

CHIEF (*sadly*). I'd never have expected this of you. Stop fighting the government? Become a conformist? You're a fine one to talk like that. The oldest prisoner in the country.

PRISONER. Exactly, Colonel. Is it true that I am the last man still in prison?

CHIEF (*hesitatingly*). Yes ...

PRISONER. You see? Some time ago it became obvious to everyone that we have the best political system in the world. My former colleagues confessed their guilt, received their pardon and went home. Now there's nobody left to arrest. I am the last remaining revolutionary; but what sort of a revolutionary? In my heart of hearts I'm a stamp collector.

CHIEF. That's what you say now, but who threw the bomb at the general?

PRISONER. Ancient history, Colonel. And the bomb didn't even explode. It's not worth raking that up.

CHIEF. Honestly, I can't believe my ears. For ten years you've refused to make a statement. You've held out splendidly. Time and time again you've been ordered to sign, but you never broke down. Instead you would stand up in disgust and spit at the picture (*gets up from his chair and stands to attention*) of our Infant King and his Uncle the Regent. (*Sits down.*) We've got used to living here together. Everything's nicely settled and now suddenly you want to destroy it all.

PRISONER. I tell you, there's just no point. If only I hadn't been so ideologically abandoned perhaps I could have gone on longer. But to think that the whole population of our beautiful, peaceful and fertile country has for so long been singing the praises (*gets up and stands to attention*) of our Infant King and his Uncle the Regent, that all the prisons are empty and that I alone, just me ... No, Colonel, I promise you. I've given up my former beliefs. If the whole people supports the government and is against me, then there must be something in it. In fact, we've got a very good government, and that's that.

CHIEF. Hmmm ... hmmm ...

PRISONER. I beg your pardon?

CHIEF (*gets up and adopts an official tone of voice*). While accepting with sincere joy and satisfaction the prisoner's confession, bearing witness to a change of heart which has come about under the corrective influence of imprisonment, I nevertheless consider it my duty to ascertain to what extent his new, favourable and entirely rational opinions are deep-rooted and lasting. (*Sits down. In a different tone.*) Why then, if I may ask, do you consider that our government is good?

PRISONER. You've got eyes, Colonel. Never before in history has our country reached such a high stage of development. You know, sometimes I move my plank bed against the window of my cell and put my latrine bucket on top of it upside down; then I can stand on the bucket on tiptoe and gaze out at a most beautiful meadow. Every spring it bursts into flower with different coloured blossoms. Then at haymaking time the farm workers come to the meadow and cut the grass. During the last ten years I have watched their faces light up with a happiness and satisfaction which grows in strength every year.

CHIEF. Do you realize that it is against the prison rules to look out of the window?

PRISONER. But for ideological purposes, Colonel, in the cause of corrective education. And that is not all. On the other side of the meadow there's a small hill, and on the other side of the hill during the last seven years an industrial building has been constructed. I can see a chimney, and sometimes there's smoke coming out of it.

CHIEF. To be strictly accurate I think I should tell you that that is a crematorium.

PRISONER. Why should they always bury dead people in the ground, like they've been doing for centuries and centuries? Don't atheists have the same right as believers to dispose of their bodies in the way they wish, with the sort of funeral they like. What you say only confirms what I've always felt, that this country of ours is a land of the broadest tolerance, even in religious matters.

CHIEF. Yeees ...

PRISONER. Take culture and art. The hours I've spent walking up and down my cell – down the length of it, that is, because it's rect-angular – all the time getting more and more excited.

CHIEF. Well yes. You've got to admit it.

PRISONER. You see, I'm right.

CHIEF. I am a civil servant and I can't settle this matter myself. That is to say I can't accept your change of heart too readily. I must first of all investigate that there are no doubts or hesitations left in your mind. It may be you are looking at things through rose-tinted spectacles. Take the economic situation, for example, are you not overlooking certain specialized matters like, say, the railway?

PRISONER. Even the most fanatical enemy of our state system could not deny that the railway, as a phenomenon, exists in this country.

(*Pause. The* CHIEF OF POLICE *and the* PRISONER *look at each other. The* CHIEF OF POLICE *gets up, walks out from behind his desk and marches up and down the room in silence. Then he stops. For a moment he gazes at the pictures of the Infant King and his Uncle the Regent. The* PRISONER *watches him the whole time.*)

CHIEF. Yes, and what about them? (*Points to pictures.*) I suppose you never had the slightest intention of ... (*Impatiently.*) No, really! It's impossible!

PRISONER. I don't understand, Colonel.

CHIEF. Honestly, talking to you anyone would think you threw a tomato at the general, not a bomb, and that it never entered your head that (*stands to attention*) our Regent, the Uncle of our Infant King, is an idiot. (*Stands at ease.*)

PRISONER (*leaping to his feet in indignation*). Colonel!

CHIEF. No, all right, that's enough, obviously he isn't. (*Goes on walking up and down.*) That is to say, as far as his intellect is con-cerned. But you must admit that even the most powerful brains have their little weaknesses; lower down, that is, among their habits, tastes.

(*He gets up, stares at the* PRISONER, *and winks at him. The* PRISONER *does not react. The* CHIEF OF POLICE *comes nearer, winks again very meaningfully and emphatically, moving his whole head and even his neck, as if he wanted to throw his eye at the* PRISONER. *The* PRISONER *turns round as if the wink were directed not at him, but at someone behind him. Pause.*)

PRISONER. Why are you winking at me, Colonel?

CHIEF (*violently unbuttoning his tunic collar*). You ought to be ashamed of yourself! You, an old revolutionary, asking such a question.

PRISONER. It's all this educational effect of prison life that you were talking about. I give you my word, I've simply forgotten what that wink might mean. Is it some sort of an allusion? Is it something unpleasant connected with the persons of our Infant King and of his Uncle the Regent?

CHIEF. You don't think, then, that our Regent is – an old pervert?

PRISONER. Him? That pure old man?

CHIEF (*again starts walking round the room*). All right, very good ... As representative of the High Command I congratulate you on your progress. (*Offers his hand which the* PRISONER *takes.*) But this does not mean that we can give ourselves up to a sudden burst of re-joicing. It is a matter of great concern both to you, since you have undergone what we hope is a genuine change of heart, and to me, who must not accept your story too trustingly. You say that you do not believe that our Regent is a – a you know what. But psychologists tell us that often a man gives the impression that he is not thinking something, while in fact he is thinking it all the time. What have you got to say to that?

PRISONER. You're right, Colonel. That's exactly the point. Sometimes it seems to us that we think we're not thinking, but we are thinking – while all the time we're not thinking at all. Thought is a powerful weapon, Colonel.

CHIEF (*pompously, sternly, suspiciously and testingly*). But only in the service of mankind!

PRISONER. That is true.

CHIEF (*unwillingly*). Very well. Now please take a look at this picture of our Infant King. Small, isn't he?

PRISONER. Like all children.

CHIEF. You mean he's a shortarse, eh?

PRISONER. You know, Colonel, if it wasn't for your uniform and high rank I might begin to think that you were right. But if the Chief of Police himself says that our Infant leader is a shortarse, then obviously such an opinion could never, never be the right one. If a shopkeeper had told me that, or a bricklayer out in the street, perhaps I'd have had my doubts. But the Chief of Police! No, this only confirms me in my great admiration and reverence for the person of our Infant King and – as a natural consequence – of his Uncle the Regent.

(*The* CHIEF OF POLICE *sits down again. Then the* PRISONER *gets up, walks towards the desk and takes up the initiative.*)

Please believe me. I've finished with my former mistaken anti-government point of view. The reasons for my change of heart fall into two categories: there are the external ones and the internal ones, and it is this double conviction which is the guarantee of the depth and permanence of my evolution – a thing which you, Colonel, for my own good are naturally concerned about. The external reasons are those we've already mentioned: the universal progress that our country has made. You only have to pick up a newspaper to be convinced of it. Look around you, Colonel. Don't hide your head in the sand in the face of these achievements. Is there anything wrong with the country? You've only got to look at your salary, Colonel, that in itself is enough to show how groundless are complaints of this sort. Anyway, I've become a keen government supporter, and I don't mind admitting it.

(*The* PRISONER *sits down and pulls his chair up nearer the desk. His tone is more confidential.*)

However, if you have any doubt that the emotions of nature are strong enough to make sure that I won't go back on my conversion, I'll show you that there are other emotions, internal emotions, which I feel more personally. You see, when I was a child I had no idea about law and order, about discipline and having an aim in life. All the time it was freedom and freedom. This – sort of – monotony in my spiritual diet could only satisfy part of my personality. Feelings of revolt against the established order, a desire to oppose all restrictions and authority – I had plenty of those. But in the course of time I began to feel a certain dissatis- faction. I came to the conclusion that I was in some way handi- capped. I, a free rebel, a model revolutionary, began to feel a curious nostalgia. How is this? I asked myself. Why has Fate tor- mented me, deprived me of the joyful sensation of agreement, subservience and loyalty, the delightful feeling of unity with authority, the blissful capacity to carry out political inevitabilities, as well as the added delight of, without needing to be summoned by these inevitabilities, yielding myself up to them voluntarily, and having at the same time a complete, self-elevating confidence in myself as a man of action? I was a man unfulfilled, Colonel, but at last I understood that it was not too late. And it was then that the time came when my first me, rebellious and always com- plaining, perished as a result of over-indulgence, and a second me awoke, with a loud voice demanding the nourishment that was its due – a joyful and calm conformity, an eager hope in the future, and the peace which flows from full submission to author- ity. The joyful knowledge that the government of our Infant King and his Uncle the Regent (*both stand, then sit*) is just as good, wise and virtuous as we ourselves, arouses within us feelings of sheer delight unknown to those poor individuals, so imprisoned in their own negative outlook and so unfulfilled in their relation- ship with mankind. Only now, Colonel, have I achieved real fullness. So here I am – the last political prisoner in a country that is now flourishing and entirely loyal; the last dark cloud in the blue sky of the rule of our Infant King and his Uncle the Regent; one single crow, with the blackness of his wings marring the pure rainbow of our statedom. It is only on my account they still keep the police force going. If it wasn't for me they could send all the judges and guards off home. The prison would stand empty and could be turned into a preparatory school. Because of me, Colonel, you've got to hang around in this stuffy office. Otherwise you could get out far into the fields and meadows with a gun or fishing rod and throw off your suffocating uniform. I tell you, Colonel, you've won at last. The police have brought their mission to a close. The last man to oppose the government lays down his arms and his only desire is to join the chorus of citizens singing hosanna to our Infant King and his Uncle the Regent. For the first time in the world's history the ideal of law and order in a state has been achieved. When I leave here the last obstacle will be gone. Today should be a great occasion in your life, Colonel. It is the day of final victory. The task at which you have laboured your whole life and for which you were ordained has been crowned by success. Today I sign the paper that you have been trying to persuade me to sign for ten years. I will then go out into the free world and support the government. What is more, I will send an open letter to our Infant King and his Uncle the Regent – the most humble letter that has ever been written, filled with the deepest devotion and love.

CHIEF. You remember that stamp collection you were so proud of?

PRISONER (*startled*). Yes, what's that got to do with it?

CHIEF. Just reflect for a moment whether you really want to leave us. Perhaps you could think it over once more and strengthen your convictions. Look before you leap, as they say. Meanwhile we could give you a hand in your stamp collecting. We've got secret agents in many interesting foreign countries who send us reports. We could soak the stamps off and give them to you for your album. Outside it's not so easy to get good stamps.

(*Enter a* POLICEMAN.)

POLICEMAN. Sir, the sergeant's back.

CHIEF. Tell him to come in.

(*Enter the* SERGEANT. *He is broad and red-faced, with moustaches twice as long as the others. He has one black eye and is limping. He comes to attention before the pictures of the Infant King and his Uncle the Regent and then flops into a chair. He is wearing a raincoat and a green hat with a narrow brim.*)

Well, Sergeant, how did you get on? My God! You look a sight! What happened?

(*The* SERGEANT *groans.*)

Does it hurt?

(*The* SERGEANT *nods his head, takes out a handkerchief and applies it to his eye. The* CHIEF OF POLICE *motions to the* POLICEMAN *to leave the room.*)

You can tell me now.

SERGEANT. Sir, as part of my duties as agent-provocateur I was trying to shout anti-government slogans – and they beat me up.

CHIEF. Who beat you up? No, you don't really mean that they ... you were beaten up by ...

SERGEANT. Unfortunately, yes. I was beaten up by the loyal population.

CHIEF (*mutters gloomily to himself*). I expected as much.

PRISONER. You see, Colonel. It bears out my theory.

CHIEF (*sharply*). Please don't interfere. Give me the details, Sergeant.

SERGEANT. Sir, immediately upon receiving your instructions I proceeded to carry them out. First of all I acquired a civilian suit, although if there's one thing I hate it's civilian clothes. To improve my disguise I obtained a green hat with a narrow brim, and a raincoat. I then went out into the street. For a short time I conducted myself defiantly opposite the government office of weights and measures, but nobody paid any attention. So I went to the square and made faces in front of the statue of our Infant King and his Uncle the Regent. (*Gets up, sits down.*) Again nobody saw me because, as you know, Colonel, everybody's in a hurry there. Then I went off and stood in a queue at a kiosk where they were selling beer. I looked around and saw that in front of the kiosk and all around me there was a collection of simple, ordinary citizens, in the thirtieth or thirty-eighth wage bracket, I should say. 'This is fine,' I thought to myself. The queue moved forward

and all the time I was wondering what to do about it. At last I had
an idea, and when my turn came I said to the man in my normal
voice, 'Two half pints, please, in quick succession.' You see,
Colonel, as if it was the royal succession that had brewed the beer,
or something, and they were giving short measure, etc., etc.
Well, either he didn't understand – he looked pretty stupid – or
else he didn't want to understand – anyway he just asked me:
'Mild or bitter, sir?' So then I let him have it straight. I said to
him: 'Our whole farming system's down the drain, and anyone
who doesn't steal will die of starvation.' Then the people who
were standing in the queue with me came in closer and one of
them asked if I was making any allusion to life in the present day,
because he was an employee of the state, and he would not tole-
rate the state being insulted. So then I gave them the lot: the
agricultural situation, foreign trade, then a few words about the
police, especially the secret police. Then a young man in a cloth
cap came out of the group and walked towards me. 'You leave
our police alone,' he says. 'I suppose next thing you'll start on the
army; you'll want to cut down national service or get rid of it
altogether, and next autumn I'm due to go before the recruiting
board.' And then some old bag who was standing a bit farther
off yelled out: 'Oh, so he doesn't like the police, eh? Why only
last week they sent me a summons to arrange to have my house
searched, and this so-and-so's going to get in the way, I suppose.
After a search you always feel more comfortable and loyal, and
if you don't have your house searched you get an uneasy feeling.'
I realized things were hotting up. But you know me, Colonel, I've
been in the police since I was a child, and this job as agent-provocateur, it's something sacred to me, although it's hard work
and, as I say, I'm sick of wearing these civilian clothes. Anyway,
I didn't pay any attention and went on with all the usual things –
the income tax, the health service and then a lot of stuff about our
Infant King (*stands up*) and his Uncle the Regent (*sits down*). 'So!'
they all shouted, 'you're one of those, are you? You're going to
stand here and slander our beloved rulers.' And then they all got
together and beat me up.

PRISONER. Bravo, what a fine set of men.

SERGEANT. And you know, Colonel, when they were beating me up there were two conflicting feelings in my mind: a feeling of sadness and a feeling of joy. I was sad that I had not carried out your order, that I could not provoke anybody to be disloyal and that once more there's nobody we can arrest. But I was glad that love and reverence for the government and for the persons (*stands up*) of our Infant King and his Uncle the Regent (*sits down*) are so widespread and strongly felt by the population, as you can tell by my black eye.

PRISONER (*half to himself, enthusiastically*). What a wonderful country! Wonderful people!

CHIEF. What you need is some steak on that eye.

PRISONER. Colonel! What the sergeant has said makes me even more convinced. I desire this instant to renounce my former ideals. They disgust me whenever I think of them. I will now sign the declaration of loyalty. Can I have a copy of it please, and pen and ink?

CHIEF (*sadly*). Is your mind made up, then?

PRISONER. Nothing can alter my decision now. When I leave this building, with all its memories and recollections, I shall straight away apply to work for the state. Give me the paper, please.

CHIEF. You don't mind about the stamps?

PRISONER. Why should I think about postage stamps when I can join the service of our Infant King (*stands up*) and his Uncle the Regent? The passion of a collector is nothing compared to the spirit of service. Of what use are my stamp albums when I can give myself up to the delights of loyalty, which I have discovered for the first time in my life after such a long phase as an anarchist?

CHIEF. All right, then. I won't press you any more. Here is a pen, ink and paper. If that's what you want, you can have it. (*Angrily puts the paper in front of the* PRISONER.)

PRISONER. At last! (*Signs it.*)

(*The* CHIEF OF POLICE *takes the paper from him, blows on it and dries it. He rings the bell. Enter the* POLICEMAN.)

CHIEF. Bring his things in here. (*Exit the* POLICEMAN. *To the* PRISONER.) You have disappointed me. I thought you'd hold out longer. It was so impressive the way you never broke down ...

> (*The* POLICEMAN *brings in the* PRISONER's *things: a cape, a mask and a bomb.*)

CHIEF. It is my duty to return you the things that were found on your person at the moment of your arrest.

PRISONER. Ghosts of the past!

> (*Takes the conspirator's cloak from the* POLICEMAN, *throws it over his arm, and puts the mask in his pocket. The* POLICEMAN *then hands him the bomb.*)

Oh no! I don't want that. I've finished with that for ever. Colonel, I would be so pleased if you would accept this bomb as a present from me and as a souvenir of our happy times together. It can be a mark of the fatherly triumph that you have achieved over me. It is all that remains of the last revolutionary. You can have the mask too. (*Takes the mask from his pocket.*)

CHIEF. Just as you like.

> (*Unconcernedly takes the bomb and mask from the* PRISONER's *hand and puts them in drawer.*)

PRISONER. Allow me to congratulate you, Colonel. The last revolutionary is dead. A new citizen has been born. In your place I would order the rockets to be sent up and give my staff three days' holiday. And why only three days? From now on there will be nothing left for them to do. Goodbye all and thank you for everything.

CHIEF. Don't mention it.

> (*The* PRISONER *kisses the hand of the* CHIEF OF POLICE, *then of the* SERGEANT *and of the* POLICEMAN. *He walks out of the door. The* POLICEMAN *makes a regulation about turn and also walks out. The* CHIEF OF POLICE *and the* SERGEANT *are left in silence. Suddenly a piercing shout is heard through the window from the Prisoner who is now in the street.*)

PRISONER (*offstage*). Long live our Infant King and his Uncle the Regent!

CHIEF (*hides his face in his hands and breaks down completely*). My
    God! My God!

SERGEANT (*dreamily*). I wonder if I could provoke him to be
    disloyal ... ?

Act Two

The action takes place in the home of the agent-provocateur. On the wall are the well-known pictures of the Infant King and his Uncle the Regent. There is a wedding photograph of the agent-provocateur sergeant and his WIFE. *A door and a window are in clear view, and there are two chairs, a table and a tailor's dummy dressed in a very elaborate uniform of a police sergeant with a large number of medals. Near by is a small screen, under which a pair of jackboots can be seen. There is a fig plant, or possibly a palm, and a small table carrying a pair of dumb-bells. The agent-provocateur's* WIFE *is on stage, as is the* CHIEF OF POLICE, *who is dressed as in Act One, but disguised with a coat and hood thrown over his uniform. He is wearing his sword.*

CHIEF OF POLICE (*his hood pulled over his eyes*). Good morning. Is your husband at home?

WIFE. No, I'm afraid he's not back from work yet.

CHIEF. Not back from work? Today's his day off, isn't it?

WIFE. He doesn't like days off. What do you want to see him about?
(*The* CHIEF OF POLICE *moves into the centre of the room and throws off his hood.*)
Colonel! I didn't recognize you.

CHIEF. Shhh ... Not so loud! Did your husband say when he'd be back?

WIFE. No. He went into town to do some voluntary provoking. I don't know when he'll be here.

CHIEF. Please don't let me interrupt you. You're sewing, I see.

WIFE (*ashamedly putting down her work*). Er ... yes. It's just some gold braid for my husband's underpants. He feels so terrible in civilian clothes these days and always likes to wear some tiny piece of military dress, even if it's underneath everything. (*Suddenly changing her tones, imploringly.*) Colonel!

CHIEF. Yes. What is it?

24

WIFE. I wish you'd take him off this job. Don't make him do any more provoking in civilian clothes.

CHIEF. Why not?

WIFE. You've no idea how thin and pale he's got since he's had to go about in civvies. He can't exist out of uniform. He's withering away.

CHIEF. I'm afraid that's just too bad, madam. Provoking is always done in civilian dress.

WIFE. Couldn't he just wear his helmet? He always used to feel much better then.

CHIEF. No, madam. A helmet would attract attention.

WIFE (*in a confidential tone*). Oh yes, of course. It's such a long time since he's had anyone to arrest. He probably doesn't show it in front of you, Colonel, but at home he's become moody and quite intolerable. One new arrest would put him right again.

CHIEF (*pompously*). You can't make arrests without an agent-provocateur.

WIFE (*dully and sadly*). I'm afraid I've just given up hope.

CHIEF. *You* don't know anyone that we could arrest?

WIFE. No! All the people I know are as loyal as hell. And if there was anyone, my husband would be the first person I'd tell, just to give him a bit of peace of mind. He's always asking me.

CHIEF. Any neighbours, then? Any distant relatives?

WIFE. No. They're all law-abiding citizens. There was an old man on our street who used to complain, but with him it was the gout, not the government. He's just died, probably of being too careful.

CHIEF. Yes, nowadays it's all so peaceful, all so quiet. Tell me, how did you first meet your husband?

WIFE. Oh, that was ages ago, Colonel. He reported me to the secret police and I reported him. That's how we got to know each other.

CHIEF. Have you got any children?

WIFE. Two. But they're locked up now. Shall I get them down?

CHIEF. No, please. I don't want to inconvenience anyone. I just dropped in to have a word with your husband.

WIFE. He may be back by now. He always listens at the doors on the way upstairs. I'll go and have a look.

(*Exit. Light footsteps are heard on the stairs. The window opens and through it enters the* SERGEANT *in civilian clothes. He is carrying a raincoat and a small green hat.*)

SERGEANT. Colonel! Fancy seeing you in my house. How wonderful!

CHIEF. Psst! I'm here unofficially. I'll tell you why later. Why didn't you come in through the door?

SERGEANT. I was walking on the tops of the houses. When it was time to come home I thought I'd come back across the roofs. It's one way of getting here and there could have been something going on. Anyway down in the street it couldn't be quieter.

CHIEF. What did you find?

SERGEANT. Nothing at all, Colonel. Just a few birds. Is my wife here?

CHIEF. She went out on to the staircase. She thought you were there.

SERGEANT. She always listens at the doors when she goes down those stairs. You don't mind if I change now, do you, Colonel? I feel naked without my uniform on.

CHIEF. No, do change if you like. You're in your own home, and it's your day off anyway.

SERGEANT (*going behind the screen*). Yes, I know. But you see, I thought maybe today would be my lucky day, and I went out. I did a bit of provoking before lunch, but as usual it was no good. They just said hello and walked on.

CHIEF. Sergeant, if it hadn't been for you perhaps we'd never have lived to see this alarming drop in the crime figures. That is to say, I mean, thanks to you we now have this perfect state of law and order. I must recommend you for promotion.

SERGEANT (*all this time changing into uniform behind the screen*). It's nothing, Colonel. I just felt I had to go and try once more. I like doing it, really. (*Pause. The* SERGEANT *finishes changing.*)

(*He comes out in full uniform with sword and medals. He stretches himself luxuriously.*)

Ah, what a relief. At last I feel I can relax. Coming home from work, changing into uniform, you've no idea how marvellous it is. Oh ... er, excuse me, Colonel. (*Realizes he has been behaving a little too informally. Comes to attention.*) This is what comes of working in civvies. Civilian clothes are very bad for morale. You see, sir, I've got to take a grip on myself.

CHIEF. Oh, don't worry about that. I've got an important matter to discuss with you. Find some excuse to send your wife off; she mustn't come in here. I'm sure she's quite reliable, but what I have to talk to you about is most secret.

(*The* SERGEANT *exits. His footsteps die away on the stairs. The* CHIEF OF POLICE *takes off his coat and sits down. More footsteps. Enter the* SERGEANT.)

SERGEANT. I sent her off to get some waterproof glue.

CHIEF. Couldn't you think up a better pretext than that?

SERGEANT. It wasn't a pretext, Colonel. I really need it. My raincoat got torn when they beat me up last time.

CHIEF. Oh, all right. Has she gone far?

SERGEANT. She won't be back for three-quarters of an hour.

CHIEF. I suppose you're surprised by my visit.

SERGEANT. Just as you say, sir.

CHIEF. You're surprised, then?

SERGEANT. Yes, sir. The Chief of Police here in my house! I'd sooner have expected a revolution.

CHIEF. No wishful thinking now, Sergeant. And a keen sergeant must always be prepared for a revolution. No, I didn't really mean that. Your service record is irreproachable.

SERGEANT. But of course, Colonel.

CHIEF. Still, in your exemplary conduct there is something more than ordinary conscientiousness and sense of duty. (*The* SERGEANT *comes to attention.*) No, don't bother about that. Sit down.

SERGEANT. With your permission, sir, I'd rather do my exercises for a bit – that is if you don't mind, Colonel.

CHIEF. Your exercises?

SERGEANT. Always at this time, as soon as I get home, I do a little weight lifting or spring exercises. I must be able to cope with any situation that crops up. They're good for my muscles. (*Bends his biceps.*) You want to try them?

CHIEF. No thank you. I can see from here. If you want to do your exercises, do them.

(*The* SERGEANT *tucks up his sleeve, takes the dumb-bell from the table and returns to his place in front of the* CHIEF OF POLICE. *All the while listening to his boss he performs a few rhythmical lifts of the dumb-bell every now and again. Every now and then he checks his biceps to see if they have hardened. He then tries the other arm. All this time he is engaged in conversation with the* CHIEF OF POLICE.)

As I said, you are not only an excellent policeman. I have found that you are something more than that.

SERGEANT (*in a very disciplined manner*). Sir!

CHIEF. I find that you have given me an idea.

SERGEANT (*as before*). Sir! Yessir!

CHIEF. You put on civilian clothes, do you not, when your job requires it, even though you can't stand wearing them?

SERGEANT. Yessir! Anything for my job, sir.

CHIEF. Exactly, in other words you sacrifice your personal likes and dislikes on the altar of service to the state. But that's not important. In examining your case I have come to the conclusion that your keenness, readiness and devotion to duty are quite out of proportion to the tasks you fulfil so admirably, even though these tasks are certainly not easy.

SERGEANT. Yessir!

CHIEF. You give me the impression of a Hercules who spends his time cutting wood and carrying water. Of course, this sort of work is difficult and useful, but it is not the work of a Hercules. In you there is a strength, Sergeant, a strength which is only partly finding its outlet in ordinary work. For you are something more than a civil servant. You are inspired by the idea of order and general discipline. You are the mystic of the police force, the saint of the police. Why have you got so thin lately, Sergeant?

SERGEANT. It's my insomnia, Colonel.

CHIEF. Oh, I see. Tell me, do you have dreams?

SERGEANT. Well, I do sometimes, but they're silly.

CHIEF. Tell me about them.

SERGEANT. Often, I don't know why it is, but I dream that there are two of me.

CHIEF. Bravo! Bravo!

SERGEANT. One in uniform and another in civilian clothes. We are walking across a big field; the birds are singing, it's warm – and then I, that is both of us, or both of me, feel in my soul that I am being carried far, far away ... and somewhere out there ... and there's a smell of fresh grass, you know, like in the spring – and then I feel such a desire, such a longing to arrest someone, to arrest someone even if it's just a hare sitting under a ridge, or a little bird. Then I look, or rather we look, all round the field; we strain our eyes and there's nobody there, nobody to arrest, and then I throw myself on the soft earth, beat my head and the tears pour out. And it's then that the stupidest part of my dream comes.

CHIEF (*in great suspense*). Tell me! Tell me!

SERGEANT. Then I dream that I arrest myself. That is to say – the I that's in uniform arrests the me that's in civilian clothes. Then I wake up covered in sweat.

(*The recounting of the dream has been a severe effort for the* SERGEANT. *While he is telling it he stops doing his gymnastics.*)

CHIEF. This is very interesting, what you say, very interesting. Now, Sergeant, when was the last time that you made an arrest?

SERGEANT (*heavily, despondently*). Oh, Colonel. I'm ashamed to tell you.

CHIEF. Well listen carefully to what I say.

SERGEANT. Yessir.

CHIEF. Do you realize that we shall never have the chance to arrest anyone again?

SERGEANT (*letting the weight fall from his hand*). What did you say, sir?

CHIEF (*gets up from his chair and begins to walk about the room*). I'll tell you something else. Not only will we never arrest anyone ever again, but your son, your grandson and your great-grandson – they won't arrest anyone either. The whole police force is standing on the edge of a precipice, on the eve of a catastrophe. What is the function of a policeman? It is to arrest those who offend against the existing order. But suppose there aren't any people like that left. Suppose that as a result of the operations of our improved and reconstituted police force the last trace of rebelliousness in our people has disappeared and that they have become universally enthusiastic for the regime. Suppose that they have formed once and for all a permanent love for our (*stands to attention*) Infant King and his Uncle the Regent. What is there for the police to do then? I did my best to improve matters and that is why I advised you to carry on provoking people to criticize the government but, as you see, even this last resort has come to nothing. Not only were you unable to provoke anyone, but when you started on your anti-government slogans they beat you up.

SERGEANT. That's nothing. It's healed up already.

CHIEF. That is not the point. We are dealing here with more general matters. For a long time I have been expecting and dreading the moment which has now arrived. Our last political prisoner has just signed the act of allegiance, has been released from prison and has begun to serve our Infant King and his Uncle the Regent. I tried to keep him back; I promised him stamps for his collection; it was no good. Do you know what this means? It means that we have beautiful prisons constructed at great expense; we have a highly trained, devoted staff; we have courtrooms, offices and card indexes – and we now have not one single prisoner, not one single suspect, not one single clue to follow up. The people have become wildly, cruelly, bestially loyal.

SERGEANT. That's true, Colonel. That's a fact. I'd …

CHIEF. Soon the time will come when we'll have to take off our uniforms; and then you'll toss and turn in bed at nights, longing hopelessly for one little interrogation. Your gold braid sewn on to your underpants won't be much good to you then. Already you're suffering from insomnia, and for the moment you've still got your job. Think what it'll be like soon, eh?

SERGEANT. No, no!

CHIEF. But yes, yes! They'll take away your uniform; they'll give you some sort of sports jacket, walking shoes and a pair of flannels. You'll be able to go out into the fields or on to the water, with a fishing rod or a shotgun if you like, and enjoy your spare time exactly as you wish. You'll be able to arrest hares and sparrows, so long as it isn't the mating season.

SERGEANT. Is there nothing we can do, Colonel?

CHIEF (*putting his arm round his shoulder, warmly*). I have come to you not only in my capacity as Chief of Police, not only as your superior officer. At this dreadful time we are both of us just simple constables. In the face of the ruin which is facing our life's work we must give each other our hands and offer brotherly advice for its solution.

(*Gives the* SERGEANT *his hand. He is very much moved and squeezes it, at the same time wiping away a tear with his left hand.*)

And now listen to me. The man who can even now save the situation – is you.

SERGEANT. Me?

CHIEF. Yes, you. Pay attention to what I'm saying. What do we need? What we need is one person who we could lock up, whom we could arrest for something which could in some very slight degree be described as anti-government activity. Having several times attempted to find this man, it has become apparent that we shall not find him in the ordinary course of events, or in what we might call a natural manner. We must, so to speak, compose this man ourselves. My choice has fallen on you.

SERGEANT. I don't understand, sir.

CHIEF. What don't you understand?

SERGEANT. What I have to do.

CHIEF. Exactly the same as you've been doing all along: shout something against the government, but with this difference – this time we won't let you off; we'll lock you up.

SERGEANT. Me?

CHIEF. I assure you that the fulfilment of the task I have set you is far more admirable from the point of view of police morality than simply provoking any old citizen to criticize the government and arresting him. That would simply be carrying out your ordinary daily work. Here it is a question of fulfilling an act which is not without a certain poetry of its own, an act which belongs only to a policeman who is specially selected, inspired, pierced right to the marrow of his bones with the spirit of the police force. This is what I was thinking of when I said that I saw in you the fire of a policeman's vocation, something that is rare even among the best of us. I said that there was something in you that had not found its proper outlet, that had been eagerly awaiting the assignment that I can only now reveal to you. You are going to be our sergeant redeemer.

SERGEANT. Colonel, I'll always – anything I can do, sir – sir, I've got a headache.

CHIEF. Don't worry about that. Now change back into civilian clothes.

SERGEANT. What, again? What for?

CHIEF. You can't act as your own provocateur wearing uniform.

SERGEANT. All right, shall I change now? This minute?

CHIEF. Yes, of course, we've no time to waste. When you've changed we'll open the window so they can hear you better from the street. Then you can stand by the window and shout out something as loud as you can against our Infant King and his Uncle the Regent. (*Both stand to attention.*) Then I'll draw my sword, arrest you, and that's that.

SERGEANT. My God, but I'm supposed to be a policeman!

CHIEF. You are more a policeman than anyone else in the world. To be a member of the police and to pretend to others that you're not a policeman – that makes you a double policeman; but to be a policeman and to pretend to *yourself* that you're not a policeman – that makes you a policeman deep down, luxuriously, in the depths of your heart. We might say that you're a super-policeman, unlike any other policeman, even a double-police policeman.

(*The* SERGEANT *goes behind the screen. There, groaning and sobbing, he changes into civilian clothes. The screen is low so that his head is visible and, at the bottom, his calves too.*)

CHIEF. Before today is out I shall send a report to the general. Tomorrow morning our Infant King and his Uncle the Regent will be informed that we have discovered and arrested a revolutionary. We shall be saved.

SERGEANT (*doing up his buttons*). What do I have to shout?

CHIEF. Haven't you got anything prepared from your previous experience?

SERGEANT. Shall I say that our Regent, the Uncle of our Infant (*stands to attention*) King, is a swine?

CHIEF. That's not direct enough. It must be something strong and forceful, with no understatement, so that I can arrest you one hundred per cent.

SERGEANT. Well then, what about – dirty swine?

CHIEF. That's much better. We'll open the window. (*They open the window.*) Now – one ... two ...

SERGEANT. Just a minute!

(*Runs away from the window and takes out a brush from behind the screen. With one careful movement he removes a speck of dust from the uniform which is now hanging again on the tailor's dummy. Puts down the brush and returns to the window.*)

All right, now! (*Fills his lungs with air.*)

CHIEF. One ... two ... three ...

SERGEANT (*shouts*). Our Regent, the Uncle of our Infant King, is a dirty swine.

CHIEF (*drawing his sword, loudly*). I arrest you in the name of our Infant King and his Uncle the Regent.

SERGEANT'S WIFE (*enters the room suddenly*). Good heavens! Still trying to provoke people. Can't you ever take a rest?

CHIEF. Silence, woman! At last he's made a success of it!

Act Three

The CHIEF OF POLICE's office, as in Act One. A POLICEMAN is nailing up some garlands made of leaves or something. He is preparing the decorations for the visit of the general. The CHIEF OF POLICE and the SERGEANT are sitting opposite each other; the CHIEF behind the desk and the SERGEANT where the prisoner sat in the first act.

CHIEF. So – you've been trying to saw through the bars of your cell window. And you kicked one of the warders. This is the second time it's happened.

SERGEANT. I don't know what's come over me, really, Colonel.

CHIEF. Is there anything you need?

SERGEANT (*sadly*). No, thank you.

CHIEF. Still, you look as if there's plenty you need. You're so pale, silent.

SERGEANT. Maybe that's because I'm locked up in prison, sir.

CHIEF. Every day I send reports about you to the general. Thanks to you we've been granted funds for rebuilding the prison, recruiting new personnel and strengthening the patrols. The general has become personally interested in your case. He says you're a very dangerous man and that it's extremely fortunate I got you in time. (*The SERGEANT shrugs his shoulders.*) Don't look so glum. If I didn't know you better I might think you were displeased with all this. The general says that today he will attend your interrogation in person.

SERGEANT. He – he – he …

CHIEF. Are you ill? Aren't you sleeping properly?

SERGEANT. Not very well.

CHIEF. Are you having dreams?

SERGEANT. Now and again.

CHIEF. What dreams?

SERGEANT. I dream I'm walking through a great big field …

CHIEF. The birds are singing, eh?

SERGEANT. How do you know?

CHIEF. Are you wearing uniform or civilian dress?

SERGEANT. Civilian dress! an overcoat and plus fours.

CHIEF. And what else?

SERGEANT. I walk on and I look upwards. There's a tree. And you, sir, are sitting on one of the branches and eating cheese.

CHIEF. I am sitting and eating cheese?

SERGEANT. Yes. I am standing under the tree and you open your mouth to arrest me, sir, and the cheese falls out of your mouth on to the ground.

CHIEF. And you pick it up?

SERGEANT. No. I don't like Gorgonzola.

CHIEF (*displeased*). A very stupid dream.

SERGEANT. Yes, Colonel.

CHIEF. Would you like a drink?

(*Without waiting for an answer, wishing to improve an unpleasant situation, he reaches towards the desk, takes out a bottle of beer and glasses, pours.*)

SERGEANT. Thank you. (*Drinks. Suddenly he puts down the glass.*) No, really, Colonel, I mustn't drink with you.

CHIEF. Why not?

SERGEANT. Because I'm just an ordinary ... Colonel, can you tell me, what am I?

CHIEF. What a question! You're yourself.

SERGEANT. But what does that mean, Colonel: I'm myself? I just don't know what I am now, a policeman or a prisoner. And another thing, if I'm a policeman, am I myself, or if I'm a prisoner, am I myself, and since I must be myself, am I a policeman or a prisoner?

CHIEF. I explained all this to you at the time of your arrest. Why start all over again?

SERGEANT. It was all quite clear then, sir, because that was just the beginning and I still knew what I was – an ordinary police sergeant in the secret service. But things really started to go wrong earlier, when I was working as an agent-provocateur. Please don't be angry, sir, but I see now that it was then that it all started, and if I'd known at that time I'd have asked you to put someone else on this provoking job. It wasn't just an idle whim that I was so upset at having to wear civvies. A policeman should never take off his uniform, under any circumstances.

CHIEF. Still, it never entered your head to make a complaint. And when it was your day off you went out to work of your own free will.

SERGEANT. But, sir. It wasn't anything like as bad as it is now. I didn't have the remotest idea, sir. Even when you came to my house yourself and talked about my golden future and said I reminded you of Hercules, even then it was pretty awful, but at least I knew that I was a first-class policeman and, as you said, Colonel, far better than all the others. It only really began to get bad when you arrested me and I started my time in prison. Prison has a terrible effect on a man, sir. From the moment I was arrested everything started getting more and more confused.

CHIEF. What do you mean?

SERGEANT. Well, sir, to start with I remembered everything just as you explained it to me. Then I began to have attacks and black-outs. I got frightened and started repeating to myself over and over again: 'I am a sergeant in the secret service. I am a sergeant in the secret service', or rather in the top-secret service. But then ...

CHIEF. What happened 'then'?

SERGEANT. Then I stopped repeating it. I didn't see the sense. And it reached the point, Colonel, that ... Oh, anyway, what I meant was that I am just an ordinary ...

CHIEF. An ordinary what, damn it?

SERGEANT. Either an ordinary policeman or an ordinary prisoner, and whichever I am ...

CHIEF. Why do you have to bring out these stupid, childish arguments. This is what comes of giving responsible jobs to people with no higher education. In your place a man with any intelligence ...

SERGEANT. What I was going to say was that whichever of the two

I am I do not think I should drink with you, sir. If I am to be a policeman, then I cannot condone your drinking with a prisoner – that is to say with me, because I am in fact under arrest. And if I am a prisoner, a revolutionary feared by the general himself and by the government of the country, there again I should not drink with you.

CHIEF. Why not?

SERGEANT. Because if I am a prisoner I must conduct myself according to the moral code of an imprisoned revolutionary, and I cannot drink with the chief of police, a representative of authority.

CHIEF. Have you gone mad?

SERGEANT. No, Colonel, this is something stronger than me. Are you in a position to release me from prison? No, you are not. So I've got to stay here. And if I have to stay in prison the effect of that environment upon me becomes stronger and stronger. I've tried to fight it, but I feel that every day I spend in prison does something horrible to me – something I don't quite understand.

CHIEF. Maybe you *are* ill. Have you ever had trouble with your lungs?

SERGEANT. No, it's not that, Colonel. I couldn't be more healthy. You saw me yourself doing my dumb-bell exercises, and I only wish you could have seen me doing my press-ups. This is something quite different. Do you know that since the time that you arrested me I have started to develop certain new ideas?

CHIEF. Be careful what you say.

SERGEANT. No, sir, I want you to know about it. For example, before this I used to travel quite often by train, and I've never thought about it particularly. But when a man's in prison he becomes, I think, much more critical, and you know what I've decided?

CHIEF. How should I know? Tell me at once.

SERGEANT. That our railway system is atrocious.

CHIEF. Do you realize what you're saying? I warn you, I shall have to report this.

SERGEANT. Do make a report, sir, please. This sort of thing gets a hold on a man and he just can't stay silent any longer. Take art and culture, for example. Will you tell me, Colonel, why did we have to torment and persecute those poor artists ... ?

CHIEF (*writing quickly*). A little slower, please. What were those last two words?

SERGEANT. I said 'those poor artists'.

CHIEF. ... tists. Right. (*Taking his eyes from the paper and stopping writing*.) No, I don't believe it. You, with your record of loyal service, do you really hold these opinions? We've worked together for so many years; everything's always gone smoothly, and all the time you were ... Do you really think that things are so bad in this country? Think it over.

SERGEANT. What is there to think over? Listen: if I move my plank bed against the wall, put the bucket on it upside down and stand on it, I can see out of the window of my cell. There's a field there and just now it's full of farmers because it's harvest time. When I examine them closely I can't help thinking – and I wish you could see it, sir – what sour expressions they've got on their faces, the general dissatisfaction that's painted on them.

CHIEF. This is an entirely subjective outlook on your part. Quite apart from the conclusion to which it leads, whether they're loyal or disloyal, subjectivism as a method is entirely opposed to our party programme. I would have had to punish you even if you hadn't mentioned this so-called dissatisfaction. And besides, it's against the rules to look out of the window.

SERGEANT. But not for someone who's fighting against the government, Colonel. Someone like that would not deprive himself even of the most trivial act of rebellion. On the contrary, he would consider it part of his duty, to bring his mission to fulfilment, not to mention the satisfaction it would give him. And another thing, when I look out of the window, I can see a newly-built crematorium on the other side of the field, and that also gives me food for thought. It is a non-productive investment.

CHIEF. Would you deny atheists the right to dispose of their bodies as they like, with their own sort of funeral? If you are against religious tolerance how can you have the nerve to criticize the government's record in that respect?

SERGEANT. Those people are dead, and your argument is not valid. And even if I hadn't looked out of the window there are writings scratched on the walls in my cell. A man sits there with nothing to do, so he reads. Some of them make you think. They aren't so stupid.

CHIEF. What, for instance?

SERGEANT. 'Down with tyranny', Colonel.

CHIEF. So! That's the way it is! It's reached that stage. And I suppose our Regent (*comes to attention*), the Uncle of our Infant King (*the SERGEANT however remains seated*), is an idiot.

SERGEANT (*sadly*). I'm afraid so, Colonel.

CHIEF. And I suppose our Infant King is a shortarse.

SERGEANT. I'm afraid so, Colonel.

CHIEF (*choking with anger*). Umph!

   (*The POLICEMAN is walking round the room all this time, but not in such a way as to interrupt the dialogue. He carries in a Christmas tree, hangs garlands on it, leaves the room and returns. Everything is done most discreetly. At this moment he enters the room.*)

POLICEMAN. Sir! The general's arrived, sir.

   (*The CHIEF OF POLICE runs to put away the bottle and straightens his uniform. Shortly afterwards the former prisoner and revolutionary enters the room in the uniform of an aide-de-camp. He has no beard but has policeman's moustaches. He stands at attention in front of the door, facing the audience, with his side towards the door where the General is going to enter. The CHIEF OF POLICE and the POLICEMAN are also at attention. The SERGEANT stands up reluctantly. Enter the GENERAL in suitable regalia, with a moustache, of course. He walks up to the SERGEANT and stands in front of him, inspecting him.*)

GENERAL. So! This is the man ...

CHIEF. Yessir, that's him.

GENERAL. He looks to me like the ringleader. Have you managed to find the rest of his gang?

CHIEF. Not yet, but we're interrogating him systematically.

GENERAL. A dangerous bird. Did you find any explosive materials on him?

CHIEF. Not so far. But we haven't given up hope.

GENERAL (*gives a whistle*). Hmmm. He's more dangerous than I thought. He's dishonest. Good, straightforward revolutionaries always have a couple of pounds of dynamite on them. It looks to me as if we've caught their key man. What do you think, Lieutenant?

AIDE. I agree, sir. If he's been searched and nothing's been found on him it means there's more to this than meets the eye.

GENERAL. Oh, Colonel, allow me to present to you my aide-de-camp. I've just chosen him as my special adviser on revolutionary affairs and anti-government activity. He's an expert on that subject.

CHIEF. Sir! No, it's impossible, sir.

GENERAL. What's the matter with you?

CHIEF. Your Excellency, you must allow me to speak, sir. You have become the victim of a mistake, sir, or of a deliberate trick. This man ...

GENERAL. Speak up, man.

CHIEF. He was the one who threw the bomb at you, sir.

GENERAL. Who?

CHIEF. Your present assistant and my former prisoner.

GENERAL. Yes, Colonel, please continue.

CHIEF. I swear to you, sir, I am not mistaken. I know him well. For ten years I used to interrogate him here in my office – on this chair, sir. It is impossible that Your Excellency should have such an assistant.

GENERAL. What have you got to say, Lieutenant?

AIDE. The colonel's right, of course. I am his former prisoner. The fact that he recognized me in this uniform and with a different hair style is a great tribute to his keenness and professional skill.

CHIEF. Why, you impertinent ...

AIDE. I am your former prisoner, Colonel, naturally. But you seem to have forgotten that I signed the act of allegiance and was released. His Excellency is perfectly well aware of all this.

GENERAL. Calm yourself, Colonel. I knew it all along, really. And you can see that if I introduce the lieutenant as an expert in matters concerning the fight against subversive activity, it is not without justification.

CHIEF. But the bomb ... the bomb ... I've still got it in my drawer.

GENERAL. My dear Colonel, everybody some time has to throw some bomb at some general or other. The organism of the body demands it. The sooner you get it over the better. As for me, I have complete confidence in my new assistant precisely because he has all this behind him. There are so many people who have still not satisfied this natural urge. You mustn't be angry if I ask you, Colonel, but have you ever thrown a bomb at a general?

CHIEF. Your Excellency!

GENERAL. You see. Neither have I. And therefore, if you'll forgive my saying so, I have more confidence in my assistant than I have in you, or even in myself. I promise you, Colonel, that if you want to be thought of as the ideal chief of police, part of your job should consist of taking precautions in case I throw a bomb at myself. Have you thought about that?

CHIEF. No, sir.

GENERAL. You see. You should think about it. The person of a general is the property of the state and the government, not of the individual who holds the rank. So any attempt of this sort, even on my part, must be considered an attack against the uniform of an officer and, so, indirectly, against the state. And if ever you should have to arrest me on this account, I trust you will remember that it was I who reported myself to you and brought this vital information to the notice of the Chief of Police, and in my trial this will be considered as an extenuating circumstance. That is the situation.

(*The* CHIEF OF POLICE *comes to attention.*)

To revert to our discussion about the lieutenant I will tell you something else. He entered the service not long ago and came to us from a situation that was, I need hardly tell you, extremely different from our own. Already he has achieved the

rank of an officer. This requires some effort, as you can imagine.
We must congratulate him on his keenness and hard work. We,
Colonel, are the old guard, and have acquired our qualities of
loyalty little by little. In him a love for the government has ex-
ploded suddenly, fresh and pure, and concentrated by his long
years of anti-government activities. And as regards his quali-
fications for this present job, I can assure you that he is second to
none in combating these same activities. Therefore in expressing
your dislike of him you lay yourself open to the charge – groundless, I am sure – of being jealous of him because of his lightning
success.

CHIEF. I can promise you, sir ...

GENERAL. All right. Don't worry. I brought him here specially
because I knew we had a tricky case on our hands with this
enemy of (*stands to attention*) our Infant King and his Uncle the
Regent. It'll be quite a business, you can be sure. Shall we begin?
(*They take their places and sit down ready for the interrogation.
There is an air of expectation, as before a stage performance.*)
Proceed, Lieutenant, if you please.

CHIEF. Allow me to suggest ...

GENERAL. What, you again? You ought to be ashamed of yourself.
This aversion of yours towards our young people is beginning to
look suspicious.

AIDE. I'm afraid you're going to be disappointed, Your Excellency,
both you and the Chief of Police. The matter will be quite short
and simple.

CHIEF. Oh, you think so do you, young man?

GENERAL. I agree with the Colonel; you are over-estimating the
simplicity of the case. We know that as a result of the accused's
incredible treachery and low cunning we have no evidence of
any substance against him. The extent of his subversive activity
is borne out by his outburst concerning our Regent (*they stand,
then sit*) the Uncle of our Infant King, the outburst which immediately unmasked the criminal and became the grounds for his sum-
mary arrest. And if the criminal shouted out things like that at the
top of his voice, how much more terrible must be the things that

he has been carrying on in silence. Still, we do not possess the materials that would enable us to discover what the criminal has done. I need only mention the fact that no explosives were found on him. On what ground, then, do you consider that the case is short and simple?

AIDE. I do not intend at this time to point to any hostile acts which the prisoner has committed openly. But I can state quite categorically that such acts are to be found lurking in their full baseness in the personality of the accused, and that even if they have not yet been carried out, they exist with the same reality as if they had been carried out. For we know, do we not, that time is one, and that it is not to be divided into time past and time present? And from the point of view of the investigation it is the most clear and damning truth.

CHIEF. If you will allow me, General, two words ...

GENERAL. But of course! Please!

CHIEF. I do not deny that we have to deal with an exceptionally dangerous criminal, and that those who have been claiming that the police have nothing to do deserve simply to be pitied, if not actually arrested. It seems to me, though, that the method employed by my colleague the lieutenant is the sign of an engaging though, perhaps, over-rash belief in his own abilities – typical of the inexperienced.

GENERAL. Colonel, I thought I asked you ...

AIDE. As far as I know the criminal began his unusually intensive enemy activity after a long period of loyalty, and even of cooperation with the government.

CHIEF. That is so, my young friend.

AIDE. We have then to deal with an exceptionally dangerous individual. It is a process analogical with the one which you, General, were so kind as to outline a moment ago when you were evaluating my career – that is to say a process of contrary direction. This man, at a comparatively late age – which leads to a sharpening of the symptoms – achieved his first sensual pleasures with the feeling that he was being persecuted. As you know, this feeling gives one an illusion of one's own importance and dignity, the same, in fact, in intensity as the feeling of God-fearing loyalty and agreement with the prevailing viewpoints, although entirely different from it in its detail of course, and this is why it is so extraordinarily attractive to people who have not yet experienced it.

CHIEF. I do not agree. This man is an abominable sort of criminal, that is obvious, but I do not see in what way he is worse than other such people who ... who throw bombs at generals.

GENERAL. That damn bomb again!

> (*Consternation, muttering.* CHIEF OF POLICE *puffs through his moustache.*)

AIDE. I can assure you, Colonel, that this man is capable of throwing a bomb at three generals without batting an eyelid.

CHIEF (*impulsively, to the* SERGEANT, *in his old superior-officer tone of voice*). Attention!

> (*The* SERGEANT *instinctively draws himself up to attention.*)

Speak up now! Would you throw a bomb at the general?

GENERAL. Answer frankly and truthfully, Sergeant. Don't take any notice of us.

SERGEANT. Well – er – no, sir. Of course I might have a few strange ideas, I admit, about the railways and the agriculture and things like that; but to throw a bomb at the general ...

CHIEF (*triumphantly*). You see, gentlemen.

AIDE (*to the* SERGEANT, *pressingly*). Imagine that you are taking a stroll on Sunday afternoon and it so happens that you have a bomb with you. You've taken it from your house, though you don't quite know why. All around you there are people, beautiful women – and suddenly you see a general ...

SERGEANT. A real one?

CHIEF (*sharply*). Behave yourself, Sergeant.

AIDE. Right! The general is walking straight towards you. He doesn't turn aside, just keeps on walking straight ahead. His medals are sparkling, his jackboots are shining. You feel that now you can pay him back for everything; that such a beautiful general won't come your way a second time.

SERGEANT. The bastard!

CHIEF. For the last time ...

AIDE. Well? Well? (*Silence.*)

SERGEANT (*struggling with himself. At last, with a heavy sigh of resignation*). No, I can't. (*Everyone relaxes.*)

CHIEF. I hope you're satisfied, General.

GENERAL. To be quite frank I am beginning to wonder why you are obstructing the investigation.

CHIEF. Me? Obstructing the investigation? Me?

GENERAL. That's how it looks to me. How important is it to you that nothing be proved against this man?

CHIEF. I protest ...

GENERAL. It seems clear to me that you are trying to hinder my assistant in his final unmasking of the criminal, in his laying bare of the full baseness of the man. I warn you that I may feel it my duty to discuss your position with the Regent, the Uncle of our Infant King. (*They stand, then sit.*)

CHIEF. And for my part I should like to inform His Excellency that I possess adequate means to demonstrate to His Excellency the unprofitability of this sort of interference.

GENERAL. Are you threatening me?

CHIEF. I would not presume to do so, sir. I merely state that I am washing my hands of the whole affair and that I will accept no responsibility for the further development of the matter in hand.

GENERAL. Very well. We shall return to our interrogation.

AIDE. May I ask that the prisoner be removed for a moment?

GENERAL. Certainly. Colonel, will you ... ?

CHIEF (*rings a bell. Enter the* POLICEMAN). Take him out into the corridor. Bring him back when I ring. (*The* POLICEMAN *takes the* SERGEANT *out.*)

AIDE. I still maintain that basically the accused is guilty of a bomb attack on the general. The problem is simply that he is a man of low intelligence and has too little imagination. But I have a plan.

GENERAL. We are listening.

AIDE. In the colonel's desk there is a bomb – the same one that at a certain time in the past I threw at the general. The bomb does not work, the best proof of which is the fact that the general is still here among us. I propose that we call the suspect in and give him this bomb. We will open the door, the general will go out into the corridor, and then I guarantee that when he has the bomb in his hands and sees the general standing opposite him, all his libertarian and anarchist instincts will be aroused. Unable to resist them any longer, he throws the bomb. In this way we will acquire a dazzlingly clear proof of his extreme evil intentions and crimes in conditions as closely as possible approaching the natural.

GENERAL. But this is madness. What do you think about it, Colonel?

CHIEF. I think, sir, that your assistant, your chosen expert on these questions and an officer of great promise in spite of his short record of service, is quite right. You should not lightly reject the idea of this experiment, General, and obstruct the investigations.

AIDE. I repeat, the bomb is harmless. The detonator didn't make contact. At least, last time it didn't.

GENERAL. So, Lieutenant, you think that ...

AIDE. I am carrying out my duty and suggesting what I consider to be the most effective means of unearthing anti-government activities. I am an officer in the service of (*they all stand, they all sit*) our Infant King and his Uncle the Regent.

GENERAL. I think you may be a little bit too smart, young man.

CHIEF. As a friend of yours, General, I would not advise any slackness in your conduct of this investigation. I may tell you in confidence that in the reports which I send *direct* to (*they stand, then sit*) the Regent, the Uncle of our Infant King, I shall be forced to describe in detail your relationship with and attitude towards the police service, and in particular your enthusiasm for unmasking the enemies of our (*they all stand, they all sit*) Infant King and his Uncle the Regent.

GENERAL (*dejectedly*). Show me the bomb. I must think.

(*The* CHIEF OF POLICE *goes to the desk and brings the bomb over to the* GENERAL. *He hands it to the* AIDE-DE-CAMP *who returns it to the* CHIEF OF POLICE.)

AIDE. Yes, it's the same bomb.

GENERAL. Definitely?

AIDE. Quite definitely.

CHIEF. Well then, General, do you agree?

GENERAL. Are you suggesting, Colonel, that I'm being unco-operative? Please explain the situation to the prisoner.

(*The* CHIEF OF POLICE *rings the bell. The* POLICEMAN *brings in the* SERGEANT.)

CHIEF. You can go, Constable. (*Exit* POLICEMAN.) You are going to throw this bomb at the general.

SERGEANT. What, just like that?

CHIEF. The general will stand in the corridor and you will be in here.

GENERAL. Can't we put it off until tomorrow?

CHIEF. Just as you like, General. Shall we consult the opinion of the government on this matter?

GENERAL. Oh, no, no. I'm going.

(*Closes the door behind him. The* CHIEF OF POLICE *positions the* SERGEANT, *gives him a demonstration of how to throw and hands him the bomb. The idiocy of the situation grows clearer.*)

AIDE. Just a moment, General.

GENERAL (*opens the door slightly*). What?

AIDE. Leave the door open, please. Otherwise he can't throw the bomb at you.

GENERAL. Oh, of course. (*Leaves the door open.*)

AIDE. Give him my mask. It should be there in the drawer with the bomb. The illusion must be complete. (*Gives the mask to the* SERGEANT.)

CHIEF (*stepping back*). Ready. Right, Lieutenant, over to you.

AIDE. O.K. Now, you are strolling along ... There are beautiful women ... Over here where the colonel is standing the sun is blazing in the sky, and there (*points to the corridor*), there is the general. His medals are sparkling, his jackboots are shining, and now you think to yourself, at last you'll pay him back for every-thing. You can see the general ...

(*The* SERGEANT *throws the bomb. The lights are extinguished for a second. A flash and an explosion. For a second it stays dark and then normal light. The* CHIEF OF POLICE *and the* AIDE-DE-CAMP *stand opposite one another in silence.*)

CHIEF. I suppose you liked the general. As your superior officer he always treated you with great courtesy.

AIDE. Quite the opposite from the way in which he treated you. He seemed to ignore the fact that you have been the chief of police for years and years.

CHIEF. What would you say if I were to place you under arrest. You must admit that that little matter of the bomb is, to say the least, doubtful.

AIDE. Yes, I have to admit that. Doubtful to the extent that your part in it is extremely obscure. In that case we would find ourselves in the curious situation of mutual arrest.

CHIEF. Young man, you will go far, but not so far as you think, and not towards my position, that of chief of police, but in precisely the opposite direction. I arrest you. (*Draws his sword and arrests the* AIDE-DE-CAMP.)

AIDE. Fine. I'm afraid, though, that by acting in this way you have brought your career to a very sharp close. I must point out, sir, that your laughable attempts to charge me with the bomb attack can only turn themselves automatically to your disfavour.

CHIEF. And why should that be, my friend?

AIDE. Very simply, old boy. You are accusing me of opposing the government and of attempted murder. They will ask you where you were when that certain lieutenant signed the act of allegiance and was released from prison. What sort of a chief of police would you be if the meanest convicted prisoner was able to pull the wool over your eyes? What sort of a security officer were you if you failed to spot his little game and simply released him from custody. And if you argue that you were right to release me, because my repentance was genuine, you would be quite correct since I really was and am sincere in my loyalty and entirely devoted to the government. However, in this way you would bring to nothing your accusation against me of attempted murder, and would place yourself in the ludicrous situation of a squalid intriguer. But to return to the point. What would you say if I were to arrest you?

CHIEF. Please do not think that the police are above arrest. On the contrary, arrest is above us. It is above everything. I am a police-man with a long record of service. So, if you think that you can establish a case ...

AIDE. Of course I can. This is how I see the situation: one of the most elementary duties of the head of the police is to protect generals against attacks by bombs. And what did you do? You personally pressed the bomb into the hands of the arrested revolutionary; you personally showed him how to throw it. It's frightful.

CHIEF. Have you gone mad? The whole thing was your suggestion.

AIDE. ... Which you adopted with suspicious eagerness.

CHIEF. But only under pressure from you. It was you who wanted to do it. It was you who were so keen on that experiment with the bomb.

AIDE. But I am not the head of the police. I repeat: what is the most elementary duty of the chief of police? Any fool will tell you: to protect generals against bomb attacks.

CHIEF. But the bomb ought never to have gone off. You told me yourself it was useless.

AIDE. I've got nothing to do with it. You had no right to believe me.

CHIEF. And you assured me a moment ago that you were speaking the truth, and that you are loyal to the government.

AIDE. That is correct. I am loyal to the government. But you as the chief of police ought to know that the fact that something is correct does not necessarily have any special meaning. It can eventually have, or perhaps does have, an opposite meaning, depending on certain circumstances. You see, in spite of your record of long service you can still only understand the most primitive arguments.

CHIEF (*resigned*). All right. We will remain under mutual arrest until the situation is cleared up.

(*The* AIDE-DE-CAMP *draws his sword and arrests the* CHIEF OF POLICE. *Enter the* GENERAL.)

CHIEF. General! You're alive!

GENERAL. I'm not such a fool. I went and hid in the lavatory.

AIDE. I must point out that the Chief of Police's outburst a moment ago must be considered as extremely incriminating. The astonishment expressed in the sentence 'General! You're alive!' shows that the Chief of Police was expecting, if not actually counting on something else.

GENERAL. I'm afraid that I am forced to arrest both of you. There are two possibilities: either it was an accident or else one of you three wound up the detonator. Unfortunately, even we are not yet able to arrest accidents, so we are left with the second possibility. The prisoner doesn't count because he is already under arrest, and so I am left with you two gentlemen.

CHIEF. Precisely. The lieutenant's past record will doubtless give the tribunal plenty to think about.

AIDE. The members of the court of inquiry will doubtless see the chief of police's motives as a classic example of their type. Leaving aside for the moment the real, more serious charges that he must face, I imagine that he intends to compromise the general's assistant. It is an understandable desire, but it arises from feelings that are purely personal and have nothing in common with the service of our government.

CHIEF. I regret to inform you, General, that in the name of this government of yours I must place you under arrest.

GENERAL. Me? What for?

CHIEF. For irresponsibly exposing the uniform of a general to attacks by bombs. You are under suspicion of condoning subversive conduct. It was you who aroused my sense of duty in this matter, and that will be regarded as a mitigating circumstance at your trial.

AIDE. We still haven't sorted out the question of whether a policeman who has arrested an individual with whom he finds himself in a state of mutual arrest, like the chief of police is with me, is able to arrest a third individual, by whom he has at some time previously been arrested together with the first individual to whom he is united by the first double action of arrest.

CHIEF. Persons under arrest are not permitted to express an opinion.

AIDE. The same to you, Colonel.

GENERAL. It looks, gentlemen, as if the police now have plenty of work on their hands.

(*The* SERGEANT *has up to now been standing modestly apart from the others. He now utters a high-pitched cry and raises one arm in the air. The rebel in him has come completely to the fore.*)

SERGEANT. LONG LIVE FREEDOM!

The Martyrdom
of Peter Ohey

A Farce in Three Parts.

Translated from the Polish *Męczeństwo Piotra Ohey'a*

Characters

Peter Ohey

Mrs Ohey
His wife

Johnny Ohey
Their little son

Hubert Ohey
An older son

Daughter

Official

Tax-Collector

Scientist

Circus Manager

Foreign Office Man

Old Hunter

(off stage) { Hounds, Stablemen, Page-boys, Trumpeters

Act One: In the bosom of the family — to the arrival of the old man

The Ohey family circle. MR OHEY *is reading a newspaper which covers his face.* MRS OHEY, JOHNNY OHEY *and the two grown-up children are sitting opposite the master of the house.*

MRS OHEY (*monotonously*). You read too much. Ten years more of this reading and you'll have to wear glasses. (*Silence.*) And in fifteen years, new glasses. And in twenty years you'll be so long-sighted your glasses will be useless. It'll be terrible. When you want your slippers in the morning, you'll have to go outside, rain or shine, cross the street and look through the window to see where they are. Or worse still, you'll make a nuisance of yourself and pester the passers-by. You won't be able to find them yourself even if they're giant size with fur pompoms like mink melons on them. You won't get any help from me. (*Silence.*) Do you hear? You won't get any help from me. By then I'll be laid to rest in the silent grave, under a slab. And I don't want any complicated headstones. Just a cold simple cement plaque with a photograph and a poem. Of course by then you won't be able to read it, you'll be too long-sighted. You can look through the church railings, I suppose. And you won't be able to concentrate because of all the traffic in the street. Anyway, when do you concentrate, I ask myself. The number of times I've asked you to concentrate. I've gone down on my knees and begged you, but you're a permanent scatterbrain. (*The newspaper moves slightly.*) You know why I'm going to die before you die? Because you're not interested in me. It would take a drunk soldier pointing his rifle at me to make you interested in me. (*Pauses for a moment.*) It would have to be an officer too.

JOHNNY. Bang, bang, bang.

MRS OHEY. Johnny, stop playing soldiers this minute. Take off that beard, you're interrupting your father's reading. Daddy has to read newspapers because that's where they write how to deal with naughty children like you.

JOHNNY. Down with the infidels!

MRS OHEY. The infidels aren't here, they're across the sea. (*To* MR OHEY.) Say something to him, can't you? He'll hurt himself if he goes on playing soldiers.

OHEY. Johnny stop it and go and play sailors.

OLDER SON (*gloomily*). Have you seen the tiger, Dad?

OHEY. What tiger?

OLDER SON. Oh, don't you know about it? I'd better keep my mouth shut ...

OHEY. Don't prevaricate when you're talking to your father.

JOHNNY. Forward! Smite the heretics!

MRS OHEY. That's enough, Johnny. Don't interrupt when your father's talking to your older brother. You'd better go to the bathroom and brush your teeth.

JOHNNY. It's after meals I brush my teeth; we haven't had supper.

MRS OHEY. You can do it before meals too. Go and brush your teeth or you'll poison the soup.

JOHNNY. Follow *me*! (*Runs out of the room.*)

OLDER SON. He ought to play murders, then we'd get some peace and quiet at home. (*Exit.*)

     (*Enter an* OFFICIAL.)

OFFICIAL. Mr Ohey, please forgive me for calling at this hour, the matter is extremely urgent. Quite exceptional. Do you smoke? Then perhaps you wouldn't mind offering me a cigarette. Or maybe we could have some tea? Or possibly a clean shirt and a new coat, eh? Of course I do have my own but I'm trying to put you at your ease. I don't want you to think I'm a heartless bureaucrat. I like your flat.

MRS OHEY. The floor's a bit of a mess. You should have seen it after spring cleaning.

OFFICIAL. I am thinking of the moral atmosphere. A floor may be cleaned and made to shine, but not the character of men. Especially in time of danger before the crisis.

MRS OHEY. Would you like some gooseberries?

OFFICIAL. Gooseberries? Ah, yes please. As the crisis approaches, the weaker brethren tend to collapse ...

OHEY. What's this about a crisis?

OFFICIAL. I have been assigned the task of settling this matter as calmly and as tactfully as possible. The last thing we want is a panic.

MRS OHEY. My God!

OFFICIAL. Exactly, you see what happens. And therefore I must ask you not to obstruct me, or I may have to use force. Now, we shall prepare the ground by discussing water sports, then consumer goods, and then, according to our plan, the difficulty of maintaining self-control. And after I have calmed you down, only then will I change the subject and reveal the terrible news I have to tell.

OHEY. I'd rather you told me straight out. Leave out the sports talks – or I won't give you any stewed apple.

OFFICIAL. Very well. Sign here, please. Now – have you noticed anything in your bathroom?

OHEY. No.

OFFICIAL. No noises, footsteps, grunting or roaring?

MRS OHEY. My husband used to sing in the bath.

OFFICIAL. No fang marks in the toothpaste or holes in the soap ... scratches on the tiles, tufts of hair on the enamel ...

OHEY. No ... except once, I remember ...

OFFICIAL. Yes, what happened?

OHEY. The water didn't come through properly. I thought there was a blockage in one of the taps.

MRS OHEY (accusingly). You didn't tell me about that!

OFFICIAL. Yes, and what else? What else?

OHEY. Nothing else. I just said: 'All right if the water won't come through, it won't.' And I left the room.

OFFICIAL. This confirms our own observations.

MRS OHEY. Please, don't keep us in suspense.

OFFICIAL. It is my duty to inform you that a fearful man-eating tiger has made its home in your bathroom. Anyone who enters is in extreme danger.

OHEY (*sarcastically*). Oh, really? Ha ha ha, how interesting!

OFFICIAL. You think it's funny, do you? Well, here is the official notification.

OHEY. Department of Zoological Gardens – yes, the stamp's in order. But why should there be a tiger here?

OFFICIAL. That is not my affair. You will receive an explanation later, as the investigation progresses. All we know now is that, for reasons as yet unearthed by science, a fully-grown tiger has established itself in your bathroom. In the day-time it hides in the hot-water pipes, which are extremely suitable, of course, because of its preference for a tropical climate. Or it may hide in the geyser. Anyway, its methods of concealment, we may suppose, are based on established zoophysical principles. Anyone who uses the bath, or the bathroom, is in mortal danger. May I have the gooseberries, please?

OHEY. So if you are right, it means ... My God, my little boy has gone in there in his soldier's suit.

MRS OHEY. Oh! He looked so sweet in that uniform, and so intelligent ...

JOHNNY (*running in*). We shall not surrender!

OHEY. Johnny, did you see a tiger in there?

JOHNNY. Yes, I saw a tiger.

OHEY. Do you want a spanking?

OFFICIAL. Please do not interfere with your son's declaration. You will mislead the authorities and upset the child's character. Now then, little boy, did you see a tiger?

JOHNNY. Yes. It was sitting in the bath and it had big, big whiskers.

OHEY. I'm going mad.

OFFICIAL (*sternly*). In that case the state will look after you in a proper institution for the insane. Shall I make a report?

OHEY. No, not yet. (*To Johnny.*) Did it say anything?

OFFICIAL. In the first place I must inform you that a tiger is not able to speak. Furthermore your fantasies are liable to have a harmful effect on our researches.

JOHNNY. It didn't say anything. It purred.

OHEY. Did it bite you?

JOHNNY. Yes, it bit me.

OHEY. Where?

JOHNNY. Here, in the leg.

OHEY. Show me! ... There's no mark here at all.

OFFICIAL. I must ask you again not to exert pressure on the child.

OHEY. Leave me alone!

OFFICIAL. Also, the appearance of a tiger in your bathroom will certainly have an effect upon your future, Mr Ohey.

OHEY. What do you advise?

OFFICIAL. First of all, no bathing in the bathroom. If you like you may wash in the bidet. As for the future, you will soon be visited by our scientific adviser. And do not forget: if you disobey my instructions and sustain any injury as a result, you will have no right to claim damages.

OHEY. I understand.

OFFICIAL. I shall now leave you. My colleague is getting impatient.

OHEY. What colleague?

OFFICIAL. From the Inland Revenue. Goodbye.

(*Exit.* JOHNNY *runs jumping after him.*)

(*Enter* TAX-COLLECTOR.)

TAX-COLLECTOR. Here is your declaration form.

OHEY. What form?

TAX-COLLECTOR. For the tiger tax.

OHEY. But it's not my tiger. I'm terrified of it.

TAX-COLLECTOR. Ah! There is a close connection between those two statements. The tiger is in your bathroom and by fearing it you are in a certain sense using it, since it is arousing in you feelings which without it you would not be experiencing. The tiger is not, for example, in *my* bathroom, and therefore it would not enter anyone's head to ask me to pay a tax for it. I am in the clear. And whether you are frightened of it or enjoying it is neither here nor there. Objectively speaking, the fear of a tiger is exactly the same emotion as the delight of owning a horse, although I admit that you, subjectively, may see a difference. In short, when there's a question of a tiger tax it's you we come to, and this is absolutely right and proper.

OHEY. I don't have any money. I am poor Mr Ohey.

TAX-COLLECTOR. In that case I shall remove your lamp. (*Takes the lamp.*)

OHEY. Is this animal going to stop me reading my paper?

TAX-COLLECTOR. The science officer will be here shortly. Goodbye. (*Exit.*)

SCIENTIST (*pushing his way through the door, carrying a machine which looks a little like an ancient camera on a stand*). Would you mind helping me? I can't get my instruments through the door.

OHEY. For God's sake, what instruments?

SCIENTIST. My tiger-measuring machine. In the old days, as you know, they used the old-fashioned bamboo, but science has made great progress since then. Hold this stand please, it's falling over. That's it. Thank you very much.

OHEY. Where are you going to put it? We're so cramped in here ...

SCIENTIST. That is something we shall have to discuss. I have been sent by the Academy of Sciences to investigate a mysterious phenomenon which has taken place in your bathroom. My instructions are to stay here as long as the necessities of science demand, and to carry out proper observations.

MRS OHEY. Have you brought your own bed?

SCIENTIST. Unfortunately no. But I have brought a fork-and-spoon set and a mess tin. Will you please assign me a room as close as possible to the bathroom. I must establish a favourable look-out point.

MRS OHEY. The nearest one is my daughter's room. But I really don't think you ought to ...

SCIENTIST. Social conventions must give way before the problems of nature. Who knows that tomorrow or the next day these same tigers will appear in the bathrooms of thousands of simple, ordinary folk. We must have the scientific data to deal with such an eventuality. Anyway, as a child I attended a co-educational school and the mystery of sex is not, for me, a matter of emotion.

MRS OHEY (*to her* DAUGHTER). Show the professor to your room.

SCIENTIST. Thank you in the name of science. (*To her* DAUGHTER.)

You may call me by my first name. Will you please help me carry the apparatus? (*Exit.*)

MRS OHEY. You and your tigers!

OHEY. It's not my fault. I can't even read my newspaper ...

MRS OHEY. You could have hidden behind the wash-basin and shot it. In India, you know, the English lured their tigers into bathrooms, cut off their retreat with the bath-plug and shot them like sitting ducks. And what about those pheasants on the big estates; gold and silver, the shooting guests were blinded by them.

OHEY. Your reminiscences won't help us now. We've got to make plans. Do you think we could throw it some poisoned soap?

SCIENTIST (*appearing in the doorway*). Excuse me, where can I wash my hands?

OHEY. In the bathroom.

SCIENTIST. Thank you very much. (*Automatically walks in the direction of the bathroom.*)

OHEY. Wait! There's a ... a – you remember ...

SCIENTIST. Oh yes, of course. My dear sir, you've saved my life.

MRS OHEY. I shall leave you two alone to talk.

OHEY (*taking the* SCIENTIST *by the arm, leads him slightly to one side*). Seriously, have you any idea how it could have got here? Where did it come from?

SCIENTIST. There are various theories: autogenesis – evolution, perhaps. Evolution would postulate the development of certain species of highly developed toothpastes into one of the greater or lesser carnivores. However, the most likely theory is that Nature at certain moments in her immeasurable existence grows tired of the strange, though logical, rules which she obeys. At such times we see the moment of Nature's internal collapse and loss of responsibility, a period in which Nature involves herself in her own senses and does not control the course of outside events. It is then that we have such startling affairs as this one.

OHEY. Yes, fine. But what if it starts breaking up the flat? Shall we sprinkle drawing-pins on the floor, or something? I do feel responsible, in spite of everything.

SCIENTIST. We have been studying this question in our Institute. The possibility of the tiger leaving the bathroom and penetrating into the apartment is very slight. It is a wild animal and does not like man, so there is no reason why it should willingly expose itself to a meeting with human beings. Besides, it is now used to the slippery bathroom tiles; it likes the poetry of the glistening taps, the bubblings of the pipes, the noises in the walls and the musically-tumbling drops of water. It would hate to be suddenly transported to the cold, rigid atmosphere of a drawing-room or the ugly bustle of a kitchen. However, our specimen may be insensitive to these external influences: it may be less a tiger of thought and more a tiger of action, in which case it might conceivably leave the bathroom and take a walk into the interior of the apartment – with varying aims in mind.

OHEY. What shall we do, then?

SCIENTIST. Under laboratory conditions we should oppose it. Nevertheless science admits that on practical grounds this is inadvisable. Science still does not possess any experimental data which would permit the drawing of conclusions.

OHEY. Does it stay in there all the time?

SCIENTIST. This is important. It spends most of its time dozing or pacing up and down by the door and it is also very fond of rolling in the bath. But there are occasional days, or even nights, when it is not in the bathroom at all. It may hide in the plumbing, or it may even go away for a short time, but it always returns and it is then that it is at its most dangerous. It is terrifying. Nobody knows what brings it to this degree of enragement – it may be the low swish-swish of a brush rasping against a set of false teeth, or the splash of water when a leg is drawn out of a bath and deposited on a plastic mat. But it is at these times that the majority of accidents occur.

OHEY. Is there nothing we can do? Couldn't we splash water in its face?

SCIENTIST. A wet tiger is even more dangerous than a dry one.

DAUGHTER (speaking from her room, which is now the observation room). Professor!

SCIENTIST. Excuse me. I must return to my instruments. But let me suggest a method of hunting the animal. It is the most dangerous but also, I think, the most effective. Profiting from the momentary absence of the tiger, the verification of which may itself claim a number of victims, one of the hunters must undress and, quite unconcernedly, fill the bath with water and begin to bathe himself. Meanwhile a second hunter hides himself under a bathrobe and waits. To increase the element of surprise, another good idea is to smear the gun liberally with soap. Suddenly the tiger appears, roaring with anger. The hunter fires!

DAUGHTER. Professor!

SCIENTIST. Excuse me. I must go. (*Knock at door.*) I see you have another guest. (*Exit.*)

OHEY. He's gone to conduct his experiments. What a shame. There were still things I wanted to ask him.

(*Enter* CIRCUS MANAGER.)

CIRCUS MANAGER. Good afternooon, sir, and how is our tiger?

OHEY. You know about it?

CIRCUS MANAGER. Certainly. I have to keep myself informed. I am the director of an entertainment enterprise – I will not say a circus until I know what your attitude is to such spectacles. I am interested in the tiger.

OHEY. My dear sir, take it! It's yours. Any time you like.

CIRCUS MANAGER. That is impossible, as you well know. But since it is here, there are means whereby we can channel it to serve some useful purpose. Our circus is not large, and until now we have never had any really important animals – just a couple of rabbits out of a hat, or a donkey, perhaps. There has never been any question of man-eaters. This tiger will put us right on our feet.

OHEY. You're welcome to it.

CIRCUS MANAGER. I have the opportunity to present a completely new type of circus performance. It will depend not so much on the tiger itself as on the tiger's whereabouts.

OHEY. What is your idea?

CIRCUS MANAGER. To bring the entire show into your apartment.

OHEY. What do you mean?

CIRCUS MANAGER. We shall create a hitherto unknown type of entertainment: an ordinary circus, with a full-feature many-act programme, performing its attractions within the walls of a simple family home. Do you understand? Who can fail to be touched by the poignancy of a family living closely and inseparably with the bright lights and glitter of a circus? Our undertaking will combine both interior and exterior, both surface and depth. You provide the house and the family, and I the circus. People adore to penetrate into a place where they are normally forbidden to enter. And so, joining together the attractions of the arena with the intimacy of a family dwelling, we shall achieve our success. At the climax of the performance the audience will be allowed a peep through the keyhole at the tiger in the bathroom. The general public, not being forced to live with this terrifying feline, will take a real delight in squinting at it for a moment and then returning home.

OHEY. Well, I don't know, I like my privacy and ...

CIRCUS MANAGER. Do not misunderstand me. The circus I am speaking of may have a slight air of degeneracy – intangible, indeterminate, but still perceptible – which will attract people to us in their thousands. But from the point of view of decency it will be quite beyond reproach. It will not be based on licence or excess, but on one specific situation. What do you say?

OHEY. Well, even so, don't you see that a whole circus in one house would be a terrible responsibility for the host?

CIRCUS MANAGER. You are still considering the matter in the wrong context. There will be no necessity for your wife to prepare two thousand sandwiches twice daily – so long as we don't have any matinées that is – and there is no need for her to greet each of our two thousand visitors personally. On the contrary, the normal domestic situation must be preserved as closely as possible; the warm, intimate atmosphere of the home will make the contrast even greater. And let us not forget that the tiger will be fulfilling its role as well.

OHEY. And *you* must not forget that this is not an ordinary tiger but a bathroom tiger. Are you sure it's suitable for the purpose you have in mind?

CIRCUS MANAGER. I never thought of that. Still, I should not imagine there would be any fundamental rules of nature which would ...

OHEY. As it happens we have an expert on the spot, and I am sure he will reject your plan. I liked my flat just as it was before. (*Knocks on door of observation room.*) Er, Professor, hello, Professor!

CIRCUS MANAGER. Hello!

(SCIENTIST *opens door slightly, wearing a shirt and no shoes.*)

OHEY. The circus manager wishes to know whether the tiger would like being watched every evening by several thousand people.

SCIENTIST. Yes, undoubtedly. One characteristic of the tiger is its sense of vanity and self-importance.

OHEY. Thank you.

CIRCUS MANAGER. The slight element of danger will stimulate the audience's imagination, although in practice, of course, the door will be shut and bolted and there will be no risk at all. So may I count on your agreement?

OHEY. Well, I ...

CIRCUS MANAGER. Just imagine how this show will enrich your experience and imagination. Have you never longed, as a child, to possess a circus? Now you will be able to enjoy all its privileges and customs and peculiarities without even leaving your home. Every evening the excitement and glare of the lights, and all in the peace and quiet of your home, with no inconvenience to yourself. At night you will lie in bed with your wife. All is calm and silent, but at the same time a performance is in progress. High above your bed they have fixed a tight-rope, and along it, step by careful step, just under the ceiling, walks our most beautiful tight-rope dancer, the star of our company. And think of your children. If only for their sake, you must have the clowns in your home. A few men jumping up and down and making faces – think what a joy for the little ones, and what a help to their upbringing.

OHEY. Yes, if I agree, it will be for the children.

CIRCUS MANAGER. Professor!

OHEY. Why do you want him?

CIRCUS MANAGER. I want to ask whether we could dress the tiger up in a Roman helmet with feathers. That is the custom in our circus. Professor!

OHEY. Professor!

SCIENTIST (*opening the door slightly, wearing a nightshirt*). No, you can't. (*Closes door.*)

CIRCUS MANAGER. What a pity. Oh well, until tomorrow I shall leave you ...

OHEY. May I make one request: please, no knife-throwing acts in the programme. I have an irrational hatred of them.

CIRCUS MANAGER. Very well. I agree. (*Exit.*)

> (*For a moment* OHEY *is alone on the stage. He walks up to the door of the observation room and knocks on it timidly. No answer. The* OLD HUNTER, *bearded, enters from the other side. He is wearing an enormous fur hat and puttees, and carrying a long flint-lock rifle. He stands by the door and waits for* OHEY *to catch sight of him. At last* OHEY *sees him. He gives a sudden start, controls himself and makes up for his confusion by the severity of his tone.*)

OHEY. What are you doing here?

OLD HUNTER. I come from Siberia, from the river Amur. I look for *him*.

OHEY (*to himself*). Fantastic! (*To the* HUNTER.) And why have you come?

OLD HUNTER. I never give up. I smell out the tiger. He is here, I know.

OHEY. Oh, I see, the tiger. It's in the bathroom.

OLD HUNTER. Never mind. I wait. He won't escape the old man.

OHEY. All right, sit down and keep quiet.

OLD HUNTER. No, I stand. And I wait.

OHEY (*hysterically*). Sit down! Sit down this instant!

OLD HUNTER. Remember the old Russian proverb: 'He who stands, shall stand.' I shall stand, my friend, my friend, I shall stand ... stand ...

Act Two: The Messenger of Destiny

MR *and* MRS OHEY *are in twin beds, side by side. From inside the apartment we can hear the noise of children's voices and of a teacher leading a conducted tour. The* OLD HUNTER *is standing motionless in a corner.*

TEACHER (*off-stage*). Quiet, children, quiet. Now form up into pairs.

OHEY. I had to let them in. Orders from the education department.

MRS OHEY. Never mind. It'll soon be night-time.

TEACHER. During our tour we shall study everything there is to know about the tiger.

OHEY. I didn't want to. They said: 'You aren't rejecting us you're rejecting the children. Most important, education means children.' I had to agree. My conscience, you see.

TEACHER. ... the tiger prefers to dwell in blocks of flats. The number of rooms in the flat is unimportant, so long as there is a bathroom. If possible, of course, it should be a good bathroom.

OHEY (*sadly*). Then more people started coming; they started bringing coach tours from miles away. They're going to put a bar in the hallway.

TEACHER. Tigers do not eat vegetables, so if the flat-dwellers wish to grow potatoes in window-boxes, they may do so without fear.

OHEY. It's gone too far. Where is that Old Hunter? All these people, all over the place.

MRS OHEY. There he is, standing in the corner.

OHEY. Doesn't he ever sit down?

MRS OHEY. No, never.

OHEY. What about the Professor?

MRS OHEY. Still making observations. You know, I've been thinking. I think it's something about me that made the tiger come and live here.

OHEY. What do you mean?

MRS OHEY. I mean ... there must be something in me that excites this king of the tropic night.

OHEY. What are you talking about?

MRS OHEY. For long I have suspected it, and felt it. The palm-tree is my cousin, the orchid – my brother. And between us there is the call of the wild, of the blood. What matter, that he is in the bathroom and I am here ...

OHEY. No! Not you as well! Don't leave me!

MRS OHEY. I have been blind. I have not known of the passion boiling within me. But now I see that my heart beats the beat of the tom-toms. It is a jungle beat.

OHEY. Think of our children!

MRS OHEY. It is the beat of the enchanted grove, dark and mysterious, but luring and bewitching. And you never said one word to me about it!

OHEY. No, please, I promise you, I didn't have the time. I wanted to tell you, but I was always busy. How can you be certain of all this?

MRS OHEY. From now on, no more floor-polishing. Instead, I shall put tiger-lilies in my hair and fling myself into torrid rhythms.

OHEY. Please, I ...

MRS OHEY. Do not touch me, you stunted northerner!

OHEY. As you wish. (*Knock at door*.) Who is it now?

FOREIGN OFFICE MAN. It's me.

OHEY. Don't come any closer. I can't bear it. Who are you?

FOREIGN OFFICE MAN. I am the Deputy Under-Secretary from the Foreign Office.

OHEY. Is it about the tiger?

FOREIGN OFFICE MAN. Unfortunately, yes. I shall not keep you long.

OHEY. Please lie down.

FOREIGN OFFICE MAN. I shall occupy the end of the bed, if I may. (*Sits*.) I have been asked to deliver a personal request to you from the Minister of Foreign Affairs.

OHEY. Would you mind moving. You're sitting on my foot. Ah, that's better. Now, what is this request?

FOREIGN OFFICE MAN. As you know, there are in this country resident representatives of a large number of countries. Their friendship, and the friendship of their various political organs, is of the utmost importance to us. There are also representatives of hostile powers, whose goodwill we should like to regain.

OHEY. Quite understandable.

FOREIGN OFFICE MAN. It is an important part of our policy to keep the ambassadors in a contented frame of mind. We try to make their life here constantly happy and enjoyable, since this has a direct influence on both the course and outcome of negotiations. Of course it is especially difficult when we have to deal with the representatives of exotic countries whose customs and recreations are not the same as our own. Recently we have had this trouble with a certain Maharajah, who hates our cold and sunless climate, has fallen into melancholy and maintains an ill humour during diplomatic exchanges. Up to now the only thing we could offer him was mushroom picking, so we have turned to you for help.

OHEY. Do you want me to play draughts with him?

FOREIGN OFFICE MAN. That is not what we have in mind. The Maharajah would recover his good humour if he was able to hunt the tiger, like he does at home. What do you say to that?

OHEY. You mean, you would like me to place my bathroom at his disposal?

FOREIGN OFFICE MAN. Not only the bathroom. The hunt must be a vivid reminder to the Maharajah of all the traditions of his country: its landscape, atmosphere, climate and customs. First of all we must have the heating in the apartment turned full on, to simulate the temperature and humidity of dense jungle.

OHEY. The flat's damp enough already.

FOREIGN OFFICE MAN. So much the better. Next, I think it would be in order to let loose a few poisonous snakes. As you know, there are plenty of them where he comes from. The Maharajah is extremely attached to snakes.

OHEY. And what if I refuse?

FOREIGN OFFICE MAN. Are you frightened of a few reptiles?

OHEY. No. But suppose I refuse absolutely.

FOREIGN OFFICE MAN. The Ministry of Foreign Affairs has asked me to emphasize the patriotic aspect of this question. There are two possibilities: either you are a worthy citizen, and as such ready to give up everything for the good of your country, or else you are skimping repayment of the debt you owe your fatherland, in which case certain suspicions begin to form in our minds. I must remind you that the Ministry of Foreign Affairs remains in permanent and close contact with the Ministry of Internal Affairs.

OHEY. And suppose I am ill?

FOREIGN OFFICE MAN. The Ministry of Internal Affairs maintains contact with the Ministry of Health. If you were an artist, of course, the Ministry of Culture would also be involved.

OHEY. In that case, gentlemen, you may hunt my tiger.

FOREIGN OFFICE MAN. Thank you in the name of Diplomacy. (*Looks around.*) What we need is a triumphal arch here and ...

TEACHER (*off-stage*). ... the tiger's skin is striped all over ...

FOREIGN OFFICE MAN. Who's that talking?

OHEY. It's a school outing. The nature-study teacher is explaining things to the children. I had to let them in: instructions from the education department.

FOREIGN OFFICE MAN. I shall communicate with the Ministry of Education. Better still, the children can dress up in national costume and present bouquets to the Maharajah. The teacher will be arrested. He is too tall.

OHEY. Are you going?

FOREIGN OFFICE MAN. My mission is accomplished and soon we shall begin. Good night. (*Exit.*)

MRS OHEY. A maharajah!

OHEY (*jumps off the bed, runs up to the* OLD HUNTER *who is still standing in the corner. Embraces him round the knees.*) Little father, please help me.

OLD HUNTER. I am here, my son, I am here.

OHEY. Help me, little father. What must I do? How can I live?

OLD HUNTER. I am no scholar. Come, we shall return to the steppe. We shall tread the mountain trail. We shall walk the path through the birch forest. Wide is our land, and ...

OHEY. What am I to do? How can I live?

OLD HUNTER. And the valleys – ai-yai-yai! And the wolves, and the bears, bozhe moy! – and the earth, and the soil, and the corn.

OHEY. Lead on! I am yours!

Act Three: Fulfilment – towards the new life?

OHEY *is bathing in a tub. The* TAX-COLLECTOR *and an* OFFICIAL *are standing next to him. The* OLD HUNTER *is in the corner. From inside the flat we can hear hunting noises – horns and barking hounds. A trapeze, fixed ready for a performance, is hanging over the tub.*

OHEY (*soaping himself and snorting*). Well, gentlemen, what is your verdict?

OFFICIAL. We are here on a mission.

TAX-COLLECTOR. We are here in case the Maharajah needs anything. We have been given an assignment.

OHEY. Hand me that brush. Thank you. So, you say the Maharajah ... er, what do you think he might need?

OFFICIAL. How should I know? A glass of lemonade, perhaps, if he gets hot.

TAX-COLLECTOR. We might fetch something for him ...

OFFICIAL. ... or hold something for him.

OHEY. And there's nowhere for him to wash. In theory we've got a bathroom, but in practice we're back in the Middle Ages. (*Knock.*) Yes, who's that?

VOICE. It's me.

OHEY. Come on in, will you? I'm catching cold.

(*Enter* CIRCUS MANAGER.)

CIRCUS MANAGER. Everything's worked out splendidly. It seems that the Maharajah is a keen circus-lover, and he has declared that the circus will in no way interfere with his hunting. We are preparing a private box for him, and a nude girl show for the finale. How is the hunt going?

OHEY. They're in the kitchen now. The Maharajah fired twice at the tigerskin in the maid's room, but he missed both times. The hounds are slipping all over the place on the linoleum. Any moment we expect the tiger to appear.

CIRCUS MANAGER. Two performances today. You remember our agreement? You must pay no attention to the audience, and you must not disturb them. I want you and your wife to feel quite at home here; just concentrate on your own little joys and sorrows.

OHEY (*grabbing the trapeze, which gets in his way when he tries to sit up in the tub*). Couldn't you have put this thing somewhere else? (*More barking hounds and hunting horns.*) They're in the dining-room now.

CIRCUS MANAGER. D'ye Ken John Peel?

OHEY. I'm not so sure.

CIRCUS MANAGER. We'll have daylight lighting. The orchestra will be by the bottom of your bed. You and your wife will be lying there, dropping off to sleep …

OFFICIAL. Can I be of any assistance?

TAX-COLLECTOR. Is there something useful I can do?

OHEY (*to himself*). What a miserable bath.

CIRCUS MANAGER. I may take it you agree, then? The royal box we shall place here, and a few armchairs over there …

    (*A loud crash.*)

OHEY. God! What's that noise, and all that barking?

    (FOREIGN OFFICE MAN *runs into room.*)

FOREIGN OFFICE MAN. Peter Ohey.

OHEY. Yes, sir. Here I am, sir.

FOREIGN OFFICE MAN. My dear Mr Ohey, a calamity has occurred. A few moments ago I, the Maharajah and a beater were advancing across open country. The sideboard was on one side of us, and we were pressing forward towards the piano. Suddenly, we thought we saw something glinting behind the bookcase: a dark object with shining green eyes. The Maharajah did not hesitate. Breathless with excitement he whispered to me, 'Now I have him.' He took his best hunting-dog, slipped the leash and growled an order. The beast leaped forward. But – the cause of the alarm turned out to be a jar of gooseberries that your wife was preserving in alcohol. The dog stuck its snout in the jar, there was a ghastly crash and the animal fell senseless. The

Maharajah is furious, and if we do not pacify him this instant we shall have the whole of India at our throats.

OHEY. And all the time I was having my bath.

FOREIGN OFFICE MAN. It is not a question either of you or of your gooseberries. The Maharajah is angry, livid, and any moment he may cancel the hunt on the grounds that it is not fulfilling its required function.

OHEY. Well please tell him I am extremely ...

FOREIGN OFFICE MAN. Angered by the futility of these lengthy proceedings and infuriated by the elusiveness of the tiger, the Maharajah has but one desire – to get to grips with that animal.

TAX-COLLECTOR. Oh dear, this is ...

FOREIGN OFFICE MAN. There is only one thing to do. Someone must enter the bathroom and climb into the bath. Then the tiger, irritated but at the same time attracted, will leave its hiding place like a flash of lightning. The Maharajah, crouching by the door or behind the geyser, will fire his rifle.

OHEY. I understand. And the man who has to go into the bathroom ...

FOREIGN OFFICE MAN. ... is you: Peter Ohey.

OHEY (*looking around helplessly*). I don't want to.

FOREIGN OFFICE MAN. This is just your personal opinion. The circumstances of the case, your sense of honour, patriotism and everything else call you irrevocably to the fulfilment of this task.

OHEY. What do you think, gentlemen?

OFFICIAL. Well, I think it *would* be better if ...

TAX-COLLECTOR. Much better.

OHEY (*to the* CIRCUS MANAGER). What about you?

CIRCUS MANAGER. From my point of view it is an excellent idea. 'Face to face with the tiger' – a superb extra attraction. And, of course, the participation of the Maharajah. The audience will go mad!

OHEY. If you please, gentlemen, before I make my final decision I should like to hear what science has to say. Would one of you be so good as to knock on the door of the Professor's room?

SCIENTIST (*sticking his head round the door, hurriedly*). My opinion is that the experiment will have great scientific significance. The final behaviour of the tiger in a bathroom has not hitherto been properly investigated. Now at last we have the chance to do so. We can make an accurate calculation of the angle of reflexion of the tiger from the bathroom tiles. (*Exit.*)

(*Enter* MRS OHEY, HUBERT *and* JOHNNY.)

OHEY. Have you heard the news? These men think I ought to go in there, into the bathroom. The Maharajah's going to shoot.

MRS OHEY. The decision must be yours. (*Clutching* JOHNNY *to her bosom.*) I only know that it is better to go than to live the rest of your life in shame. Johnny, take a last look at your father.

OHEY. So, you are unanimous.

FOREIGN OFFICE MAN. Politically speaking, it is essential that you go.

CIRCUS MANAGER. And artistically.

SCIENTIST (*sticking his head round the door again*). And scientifically.

MRS OHEY. You'll look so handsome in the bath, between the tiger and the Maharajah.

FOREIGN OFFICE MAN. I must go and inform His Excellency. (*Exit.*)

(*Enter the* SCIENTIST *with the Oheys'* DAUGHTER. *After a moment the* FOREIGN OFFICE MAN *returns.*)

OHEY (*losing his temper slightly*). All right, you win, anything you say. Only yesterday, here I was quietly reading my newspaper with my family. And now? My house is a milling ground for politics, science, art and authority. They own this apartment now, not me. Off I go to satisfy state expediency, the claims of science, the whims of the Muses and the edicts of power. It is the only way to escape their tyranny for ever. And the part my family has played in this affair I would rather forget. The room where I used to read my daily newspaper has become a dog track, and the place where I used to snooze quietly after dinner is now filled with bogus tight-rope-walking equipment. A collection of assorted elements, plots and ambitions, fevered phantoms, lack of respect for fathers and chaos have forced

their way in here. This age does not please me and I have no
wish to seek slavishly for its approval. Hand me my dressing-
gown. (TAX-COLLECTOR *and* OFFICIAL *hand him his dressing-
gown. They form a procession.* OHEY, *accompanied by the* FOREIGN
OFFICE MAN *and the* OFFICIAL, *walks towards the bathroom. The
others follow.*)

OHEY (*to the* OFFICIAL *and the* FOREIGN OFFICE MAN). Thank you,
my friends! (*Looks at them all for the last time. Walks into the bathroom. The rest all gather by the door, frantically peering through the
keyhole.*)

SCIENTIST. Move over, I want to see too.

MRS OHEY. Oh, this is so upsetting. Shhh, Johnny, go away and
play soldiers. Don't look in there. Hubert, go and change into
your best clothes. Your father has just thrown himself into the
jaws of the tiger.

SCIENTIST (*as a commentator*). ... the bathroom shines with a lustre
reflected from the white tiles. Peter Ohey, his face firm and
determined, turns on the taps. The water rushes out ...

OFFICIAL. Now he's in the bath.

CIRCUS MAN. The Maharajah, that flower of the Orient, crouches
behind the geyser. His eyes burn and his face is dark and lined.
He holds his rifle at the ready.

FOREIGN OFFICE MAN. Let me look. In the name of the government, let me look. Oh!

CIRCUS MANAGER. What is it? What can you see?

FOREIGN OFFICE MAN. The Maharajah raises the gun to his eye.

SCIENTIST. Yes, what else?

    (*Two shots.*)

FOREIGN OFFICE MAN. He fires both barrels. Wait! I can't see
anything. The bathroom's full of smoke and gunpowder.

CIRCUS MANAGER. I can see two shapes, cloudy and indistinct
against the smoke. Yes! It's the Maharajah and Peter Ohey.
They are kissing and embracing like two brothers. Just a minute.
What's this?

SCIENTIST. Let me see. How extraordinary ... (*Two more shots.*)
Both barrels. I can't see. The smoke's so thick ... Oh, my God!

EVERYONE. What's happened? What is it?

SCIENTIST. Oh, nothing, nothing at all. It's all hidden by the smoke. I think I'd better be leaving.

> (*They all look at each other.*)

CIRCUS MANAGER. Yes, it's getting late.

SCIENTIST. We mustn't overstay our welcome.

TAX-COLLECTOR. We'll be off, then.

MRS OHEY. It was such a pleasure to have you.

FOREIGN OFFICE MAN. I'll say goodbye as well. I have urgent business connected with the Maharajah's departure.

MRS OHEY. What a shame. The time passed so quickly.

FOREIGN OFFICE MAN. Your humble servant, madam. I am sure we shall meet again, soon.

CIRCUS MANAGER. There's no reason for me to stay either.

SCIENTIST. And I must get back to my work. Goodbye. (*To* CIRCUS MANAGER.) Would you help me carry my instruments? (*They carry out the apparatus.*)

OFFICIAL AND TAX-COLLECTOR. Please don't think we had anything ... it wasn't us at all ...

MRS OHEY (*huddling her three children into a group and embracing them*). Yes, children, the happy days come, and they go ...

> (*They all leave except* MRS OHEY *and the* CHILDREN, *who stand motionless. After a second the* OLD HUNTER, *who has hitherto been standing still in a corner, walks up to the bathroom door.*)

OLD HUNTER. Peter Oheyevich, are you there, Peter Oheyevich? (*Silence.*) Come, let us go to the steppe. Let us walk the banks of the lakes. Let us go far, far, for our land is wide. Peter Oheyevich, come!

Out at Sea

Translated from the Polish *Na Pełnym Morzu*

Characters

Fat Castaway

Medium Castaway

Thin Castaway

Postman

Butler

The action takes place in a single act and with a single set, which represents a raft out at sea. Three shipwrecked men, in smart black suits and white shirts, with their ties correctly tied and white handkerchiefs sticking out of the top pockets of their coats, are each sitting on a chair. There is also a large trunk on the raft.

FAT. I am hungry.

MEDIUM. I could do with some food.

THIN. Are the provisions entirely exhausted?

FAT. The provisions are entirely exhausted. There is not the tiniest morsel.

THIN. I thought there was one more tin of sausages and baked beans?

FAT. There are no more tins.

MEDIUM. What I want is something to eat.

THIN. I want something too.

FAT. 'Something'? Gentlemen, we must be realistic. What we want is more like ...

MEDIUM. I don't care what it is.

THIN. You said the provisions were exhausted. So what have you got in mind?

FAT. We must eat not something, but someone ...

MEDIUM (*looking behind, to right, and to left*). I can't see ...

THIN. I can't see anyone either, except ... (*Suddenly stops talking. Pause.*)

FAT. We must eat one of us.

MEDIUM. Fine! Let's start.

THIN (*agreeing with undue haste*). Yes, let's start!

FAT. Gentlemen, we must not be children. Allow me to point out that we cannot all join in a cry of 'let's start'. In such a situation one of us must say, 'If you please, gentlemen, be so kind as to help yourselves.'

MEDIUM. Who?

THIN. Who?

FAT. That is exactly the question I was going to ask. (*There follows an awkward silence.*) I appeal to your sense of loyalty, and to your good breeding.

MEDIUM (*suddenly points to the sky, as if he had just spotted something amazingly interesting*). Look! There's a seagull! A seagull!

THIN. I'm sorry to have to admit this so frankly, but I am an extremely selfish man. I have always been an egoist. Even when I was a schoolboy, I used to eat my lunch quite alone. I never shared it with anyone.

FAT. How very unpleasant. In that case we shall have to draw lots.

MEDIUM. Fine.

THIN. That is the best solution.

FAT. We shall draw lots in accordance with the following system. One of you two gentlemen will declare a number. Then the second gentleman will choose another number. Finally I too shall declare a third number. If the sum of all three numbers is odd, the lot will fall upon me. I shall be eaten. However, if it so happens that the sum is even, one of you two will be eaten. (*Pause.*)

MEDIUM. No ... I don't think I approve of gambling.

THIN. What happens if you make a mistake?

FAT. I am sorry if you don't trust me.

MEDIUM. We'd better find another way. We are civilized men. Drawing lots is a remnant of the Dark Ages.

THIN. It's superstitious nonsense.

FAT. Very well. We can organize a general election.

MEDIUM. Not a bad idea. (*To* FAT.) I suggest you and I form an electoral alliance. That will simplify the campaign.

THIN. Parliamentary democracy is out of date ...

FAT. But there's no other way. If you'd prefer a dictatorship, I'd be happy to assume the supreme power.

THIN. Oh no. Down with tyranny.

FAT. Free elections, then.

MEDIUM. And secret ballot.

THIN. And no electoral alliances. Every candidate must campaign separately.

FAT (*stands up, opens the trunk, and takes out a top hat*). Here is a hat. Into it we shall put our voting slips with the name of the candidate.

THIN. I don't have a pen.

MEDIUM. I would be happy to lend you one.

FAT (*taking a fountain pen from his pocket*). Here is a pen!

MEDIUM (*rubbing his hands*). Hurrah for the elections!

THIN. One moment. If we are going to arrange these elections like civilized men, we cannot leave out the pre-election campaign. Everywhere in the cultural world the campaign precedes the voting.

FAT. If you insist ...

MEDIUM. All right, let's make it quick.

FAT (*gets up from his chair and walks to the centre of the raft*). The campaign is now open. Who will be the first to speak?

MEDIUM (*to* THIN). What about you?

THIN. I'd rather speak later. I was never a good orator.

FAT. But it was your suggestion.

MEDIUM. Exactly, all this electioneering and politicizing was your idea. So you must be the first to speak.

THIN. Of course, as you gentlemen wish ... (*Stands on his chair, as if on the rostrum. The two other castaways arrange themselves in front of him.* FAT *takes from his pocket a cloth banner with two handles, one of which he hands to* MEDIUM. *They hold the banner above their heads. It reads:* WE WANT FOOD.) Ha-hmm ... gentlemen!

MEDIUM (*interrupting him*). Don't you soft soap us! We're simple people!

FAT. I quite agree. Down with idle phrases. We want the whole truth.

THIN. My friends, we are gathered here ...

MEDIUM (*interrupting him*). Get to the point!

FAT. We haven't got all day!

THIN. We are gathered here to discuss the burning question of food supplies. My friends, it would be wrong for you to consider me as a candidate. I have a wife and children. Many a time, at sunset, I have sat in my garden, watching my children swinging away on their swing, my wife knitting and the darkness gathering. Gentlemen! Friends! Can you visualize this serene, beautiful picture? Does it not touch you?

MEDIUM. That's no argument. When it's a matter of the public good, sentiment is out of the question. Your children can swing on their own.

FAT. Better, probably.

THIN. My friends! When I was a boy, I had such wonderful plans for the future. True, I did not work hard enough. I never achieved my dreams. But it is still not too late. All this can be changed, I assure you. I am not going to neglect my duty any longer. I've had my troubles, it's true – lack of self-confidence, laziness – but I shall improve, I swear it. I shall exercise my will, shape my character, acquire knowledge, and finally achieve everything that lies in store for me. I shall become someone.

MEDIUM. Louder!

THIN. I shall become someone!

FAT. Selfish!

MEDIUM. We want food!

FAT. All together now: one, two, three ...

FAT AND MEDIUM (*simultaneously*). We want food! We want food!

THIN (*breaking down, almost in tears*). No. It's no good ... it's no good ... (*Comes down from the tribune.*)

MEDIUM (*hands him his end of the banner and mounts the rostrum himself*). Fellow diners!

FAT. Hear, hear!

(THIN *begins clapping his hands, but not very enthusiastically.*)

MEDIUM. I am not an orator and I do not intend to speak for long. Action is my motto. Ever since my childhood I have been passionately interested in the art of cookery. It's not so much the actual food – oh no! I'm a man of modest appetites and quite frankly I don't like eating. All I need is – that is to say I eat very little, almost nothing, in fact. What am I saying? I don't eat anything at all. Two years ago maybe I ate a little piece here and there, every two or three days, but now? Not a thing! I've finished with food once and for all. However, the preparing of food has become the joy of my life. As a cook I know nothing more exciting than to watch other people eating what I have made with such careful effort, and enjoying it. That is the only reward I desire. Let me add simply that I am a specialist in meat dishes. My sauces are without equal. That is all I have to say.

FAT. Bravo! (*Applauds.* THIN *is apathetic, and hardly reacts at all.* MEDIUM *descends from the rostrum and* FAT *takes his place.*)

MEDIUM. Hurrah! (*He stops.* FAT *stands with arms akimbo. For a moment he looks about him in all directions, as if surrounded by a vast crowd.*)

FAT (*suddenly extends his hand in a fascist salute*). Hungry men, I salute you!

MEDIUM (*enthusiastically*). Hurrah! Hear, hear!

FAT (*silences him with an authoritative gesture of his hand*). My speech will be brief—one soldier to another. First, I do not want to influence your opinions. You must decide for yourselves. I am your servant, and your will is sacred to me. I eat what I am given. Second, there's no point in denying it, I am indigestible. I have always been weak, bony and leathery. I have two metal ribs, an amputated liver and one leg shorter than the other. Why should I hide it? Thirdly, I do not wish to be a demagogue. I prefer straight talking. If I am not chosen, I shall give the other man the rump and the sirloin all to himself. I shall be happy with what's left over, and the tongue. Let any man with aggressive intentions beware. I shall not surrender the tongue!

MEDIUM. Bravo, bravo! Long live our leader!

FAT. That's all. No more chattering or philosophy. Forward to battle!

MEDIUM. Bravo! Hear, hear! Encore! Three cheers! Hurrah!
(FAT *comes down from the rostrum.* THIN *and* MEDIUM *roll up their banner.*)

FAT (*to* THIN). Are you satisfied?

THIN. You were wonderful! Only ... it's just that ... that I can't

eat sirloin. It's bad for me. If it doesn't make any difference
to you ...

MEDIUM (*standing at attention in front of* FAT). Sir! My congratula-
tions. Your speech moved me deeply. In the matter of the
tongue I am entirely on your side.

FAT. Well, that's the end of the campaign. Now we shall vote.
(FAT *puts down the top hat in the middle of the raft. The men go
to three separate corners of the raft and start to write on their cards,
their backs turned to each other.* FAT *and* MEDIUM *snatch glances
at* THIN. FAT *creeps up to* THIN *and peeps over his shoulder.* THIN
*notices him in time and hides his card. Then he gives the pen back
to* FAT.)

THIN. Thank you very much indeed.

FAT. Don't mention it. Anything else I can do for you, I am at your
disposal. (FAT *walks off to another corner of the raft. Now* FAT
and MEDIUM *fill in their cards. All the time* THIN *is standing with
his back to them, gazing at the sea. Then they all turn round at the
same time, walk into the middle of the raft and put their slips into the
top hat.*) Now we shall count the votes.

MEDIUM. It's very exciting. Voting certainly sharpens the appetite.

THIN. You might be more tactful.
(FAT *puts his hand into the top hat. Then he raises his head and gazes
silently at* THIN. *A long pause.*)
What's the matter? What has happened?

MEDIUM. What's the result?

FAT. Gentlemen, we must annul the elections.

MEDIUM. Why? I'm hungry.

THIN. Are you trying to sabotage our free, democratic elections?

FAT. In the top hat there are four cards. Four! (*As before,* FAT *looks
suspiciously at* THIN. *So does* MEDIUM.)

THIN (*innocently*). I said parliamentary democracy was out of date.

MEDIUM. What happens now?

FAT. This is a cabinet crisis. Maybe it would be simpler to nominate
a candidate?

THIN. Who will do the nominating?

FAT. I should be happy to oblige.

THIN. Exactly. Just as I thought. No! Out of the question.

MEDIUM. A very bad business. Democracy doesn't work. Dictatorship is unacceptable. We've got to think of something.

FAT. At such moments the only one who can help us is a man of devotion and inspiration who will offer *himself*. When the normal forms of behaviour fail, it is the volunteers who so often save the situation. (*Preparing once again for an oration*.) My dear friend ...

THIN. Oh no! I won't listen to you.

MEDIUM. Listen to him!

FAT. My dear friend! We know that such characteristics as devotion to duty, love of one's neighbour and loyalty cannot be concealed. From the moment of our meeting my friend and I saw that in you there was something that separated you from us. I refer, of course, to your innate nobility, your unswerving desire to assist the common good, your readiness to ... Isn't that right, my friend?

MEDIUM (*eagerly*). In all my life I never met a better man.

FAT. We are happy that at last society can provide you with the chance to fulfil your pure, though hidden, longing: your yearning to be remembered by us as a man of modesty, loyal, warm-hearted, delightful, succulent ...

THIN. No! I don't want to.

MEDIUM. What's that? You don't want to volunteer?

THIN. No.

FAT. Will you betray your fellow men? Surely you must ...

THIN. No.

MEDIUM. That's disgraceful!

FAT. You absolutely refuse?

THIN. I refuse categorically. I have no call to greatness.

MEDIUM. I don't think I want to speak to you ever again. I thought you were a man of honour, the patriot of our raft. And you have shown yourself to be a scoundrel. Goodbye. (*Walks away and turns his back on* THIN.)

FAT. We are very disappointed. Clearly honour means nothing to you. However, maybe you can suggest some other way out? Can you?

THIN (*with increasing faith*). Yes! Certainly! The only thing I require is justice. Justice in everything – no more and no less.

FAT. You amaze me.

THIN. Why?

FAT. How can you be sure that justice will not decide against you – that is to say, in your favour, in you as a candidate?

THIN. It's quite simple. I've had such a miserable, unfortunate life. Even as a child, nothing ever worked out for me. Circumstances fought against me, so ...

FAT. So you consider that universal justice will compensate for your hitherto lack of happiness?

THIN. Yes.

FAT. It's an extraordinary thing how the only people who complain about lack of justice are the irresponsible elements. They demand justice, simply because they wish to profit from the success of others.

THIN. No, I won't withdraw. I agree to anything, on condition that the decision is a just one.

FAT. You mean on condition that you're not eaten.

THIN. Now you're making insinuations. Justice first, if you please.

FAT. Let us sit down, gentlemen. I know this is difficult, but it has to be done.

MEDIUM. I'm not talking to him. (*They all take up places as at the beginning.*)

FAT (*to* MEDIUM). My dear friend, is your mother alive?

MEDIUM (*hesitatingly*). I ... don't know, boss ... What about yours?

FAT (*raising his eyes to the sky*). Unfortunately, I became an orphan very soon after my birth. My poor parents!

MEDIUM (*hastily*). That's just what I was going to say. Quite frankly, I have no parents at all.

FAT (*to* THIN). What about you?

THIN. I have a mother. At this moment she mourns me in her loneliness. Poor mother!

FAT. It appears to me that from the point of view of justice the affair is simple. Surely it would be against your conscience to harm an orphan? Even savages consider orphanhood one of the most terrible of misfortunes. No, my dear sir, if one of us two orphans were to be eaten, it would be a slap in the face to elementary justice. Isn't being an orphan enough, without being eaten as well?

THIN (*in confusion*). But ...

FAT. No, my dear sir. It is as clear as the day. You possess a mother, things have been better for you on earth, don't you think it is now time to repay this moral debt to the orphans of this world – all those who have never known a mother's care, the warmth of a home and food in abundance? Especially since, as you admitted just now, your mother is *already* mourning your death.

THIN (*desperately searching for an answer to this argument*). I don't know, maybe my mother has died. She was feeling very weak last time I saw her. I haven't been home for ages.

FAT. Now you're talking like a child. How on earth could we prove such a thing?

MEDIUM. Yes, what about proof, eh?

THIN. All I say is she was not feeling well when I left home. There's so much talk about illness in modern civilization ...

FAT. Artistic fantasies ... pure imagination. Clearly your mother is enjoying excellent health, and may God grant her a long life. While as for our parents ... (*To* MEDIUM.) Do you remember those long autumn evenings when we were bare-footed children, wandering about selling matches to the passers-by?

MEDIUM. Please, don't talk about it. There are some things it is better to forget.

FAT. And do you recall the distant relative, the mean despot who took away our last piece of cheese because he wanted to bait a mouse-trap?

MEDIUM (*groaning*). Nightmares of the past.

    (FAT *stands silently with hands outstretched in front of* THIN *as much as to say, 'You see, there's nothing we can do.'*)

THIN. Excuse me, I thought I heard someone talking out at sea. (*Listens.*)

FAT. You're changing the subject. Of course. Human suffering arouses

no feeling in your heart. You're all the same; selfish sons of
mothers …

    (*A voice is heard, weak and in the distance.*)

MEDIUM (*accusingly*). He spent his childhood playing with toys!

FAT. That's right. Toys and teddy-bears.

    (*The same voice, nearer this time.*)

VOICE. Help! Help!

THIN. I did not! Aha, I definitely heard it that time.

VOICE. Help!

FAT. Yes, there's someone swimming towards us. Orphans always
have the worst of the luck.

MEDIUM (*standing up and looking out to sea*). It could be someone
with some food, boss. I can see better now, he's only swimming
with one hand. The other one's holding something.

    (FAT *and* THIN *also get up from their chairs and walk to the edge
of the raft where* MEDIUM *is.*)

THIN. Yes, yes, that's quite possible. A farmer on his way to
market falls into the water with his pig. And then as he swims
he uses one arm to hang on to the pig, his only possession …

FAT. There, I can see him!

MEDIUM. It's someone in uniform.

VOICE (*quite near*). Help!

    (*A* POSTMAN *climbs out of the sea, complete in his uniform, cap,
and with his leather bag slung round his neck.* MEDIUM *gives
him his hand and pulls him on to the raft.*)

POSTMAN. Thank you very much.

FAT. Have you got anything to eat?

POSTMAN. Absolutely nothing. I wouldn't mind a bite myself.
I haven't had a thing since breakfast. (*Notices* THIN.) Good God,
it's you! What an extraordinary coincidence!

FAT (*suspiciously*). You know each other?

POSTMAN. Of course we do! I've delivered his mail for ten years.
I had no idea I'd find you in the middle of the ocean. Things
have turned out very well, as it happens. I've got a telegram
for you.

THIN. Telegram for me?

POSTMAN. Yes. I was walking towards your seaside house to deliver it, when a wave washed me away. It's lucky I'm a good swimmer. (*Looks in his bag.*) Here it is.

THIN (*moving to one side to open and read his telegram*). Excuse me, please.

FAT (*suspiciously, to the* POSTMAN). Is that uniform genuine?

POSTMAN. It's genuine, only it's wet. You see, when it goes in the water ...

THIN. Hurrah!

FAT. What's happened?

THIN (*pondering*). Gentlemen, I have suffered a terrible tragedy. My mother has died.

MEDIUM. That's done it!

THIN. And while we're on the subject, allow me to point out that now I am an orphan as well as you, and therefore we must reopen the discussions and once again consider the matter of one of us being eaten.

FAT. I protest! It's a trick. You fixed it all up with the postman!

POSTMAN (*pompously*). Are you insulting a civil servant in the execution of his duty?

FAT. How much did you pay him? I suppose you were at school together.

THIN. Your accusation is quite groundless. Please ask the postman whether or not I conspired with him.

FAT. Fine. We'll ask him. If he says yes, if he pleads guilty, we'll eat you without leave of appeal. If he denies it, we'll eat the postman.

POSTMAN. What's that about eating me? I've only just arrived!

FAT. That's the reason. You must be fresh – you'll do perfectly.

MEDIUM. Boss, do you think we ought to eat both of them? One of them fried, and the other with salad or stewed fruit? Or we could marinate them, or put one on top of the other ...

THIN (*hopefully*). Maybe the postman isn't an orphan? Here we are, the three of us – homeless, abandoned ... We ought to ask him, don't you think?

FAT (*still thinking about the menu*). No, I'd rather make wine out of the other one. Only how can we make Burgundy out of a postman?

POSTMAN (*joining in eagerly*). Yes, quite. I'm a first-class postman, but a very poor Burgundy.

THIN (*to the* POSTMAN). If you give false testimony that we were in collusion, I'll report you to the department of posts and telegraphs.

POSTMAN. Don't worry about that! I have served thirty years – without blemish.

FAT. We're wasting time. Were you in collusion with this man? Yes or no? If the answer's yes and the news of the death of his mother is false, we will give you the kidneys and perhaps part of the rump. However if the information is true, then we three orphans will eat you for the simple reason that you are a postman. The post office is an institution of public utility, and as such it must serve everybody.

THIN. Please, do not destroy your good reputation.

POSTMAN. There's no fear of that. For years I have been an honest postman, I can't be bribed with a few kidneys.

FAT. We could perhaps offer you the knee-bone in addition, but I warn you, that's as far as we'll go.

POSTMAN. No, sir. (*Pointing at his uniform.*) You see these two crossed trumpets? The honour of these trumpets I value more than anything else. I wish you goodbye. (*Jumps into the water.*)

THIN. No, no, don't go away. Tell them I'm innocent first. Wait! (*Waving the telegram.*) Now, my friends, you can see, from the justice point of view our situation is identical. We are all orphans.

FAT (*matter-of-factly, to* MEDIUM). Would you please lay the table. The things are in my trunk.

THIN. What? My fellow-orphans, preparing to ...

FAT. You are forgetting that there exist other sorts of justice. For instance, historical justice.

THIN. What do you mean?

MEDIUM (*who has meanwhile been opening the trunk*). Boss, do we need the colander?

FAT. The fact that we are all without parents does not place us all

on the same level. The question must now be considered: who
were our parents?

THIN. Good Heavens, they were … just parents.

FAT. Ha ha! And who was your father?

MEDIUM. What about the rolling pin?

THIN. My father? He was an office worker. What about yours?

POSTMAN (*emerging from the sea, leaning against the edge of the raft*).
Excuse me, I forgot the receipt. All that talk about eating people,
I lost my head.

THIN. Where shall I sign?

POSTMAN. Here, please. (THIN *signs the receipt*.) Goodbye. (*Swims
away.*)

FAT. So your father was an office worker? Just as I expected. You
know what my father was?

THIN. No.

FAT. He was a simple, illiterate woodcutter. My friend, of course,
never had a father. His mother conceived him as a result of
extreme worry, poverty and distress. You see, while your father
filled in office forms as a servant of the aristocracy, sitting com-
fortably in a warm, clean office, my father was felling fir trees
for pulp, so that your father could have paper to write his notices
to quit, which he would then send to the mother of my poor
friend here, who never had a father. I hope you're ashamed of
yourself.

(MEDIUM *has been taking out of the trunk certain kitchen implements, which he places on the raft. Now he takes out a mincing
machine, which he puts to the test by turning the handle several times.*)

THIN (*understanding what* FAT'*s insinuations are leading up to tries to
defend himself in the same idiom*). But I had nothing to do with
that!

FAT. That is why the justice which now decrees that you should be
eaten is called historical justice.

VOICE FROM THE SEA. Your Grace! Your Grace!

FAT. For God's sake, now what's happening?

(*Alongside the raft appears the head of an old family* BUTLER
with hoary sideboards.)

BUTLER. Your Grace, how wonderful that I've found you.

FAT. What are you saying?

BUTLER (*almost crying with emotion*). Don't you recognize me, Your Grace? Don't you remember how I taught you to ride a pony, when Your Grace was only a little viscount.

FAT. Go away!

BUTLER. How wonderful that my old eyes should behold you once again, Your Grace. Everyone in the palace is so worried. When the news arrived that your ship was sunk, I could not restrain myself. I said to myself, where he goes, I go. His fate is my fate. So I jumped into the sea and here I am, Your Grace. What luck, eh?

FAT. John, will you please leave the raft and drown.

BUTLER. Certainly, Your Grace. What luck, how wonderful! (*Vanishes.*)

THIN. No, no, my good man, don't leave us! Come here, please ... He's drowned.

FAT (*in a tone as if nothing had happened*). As I was saying, you can see that historical justice ...

THIN (*becoming excited*). I see, do I? I see that you used to live in a palace, and you took pony lessons ...

FAT. Pony? My father couldn't even afford a Shetland pony! You're thinking about your own sordid childhood.

THIN. This is the end! Are you trying to say it was me, me who rode a pony?

FAT. Certainly. You said so yourself a moment ago.

THIN. No, this passes all understanding! I declare categorically that I have had no connexion whatever with any pony.

FAT. No more have I. My poor father didn't even know the word 'pony'. He was illiterate.

MEDIUM (*has meanwhile been watching the scene, standing over the various kitchen implements, with a saucepan in his hand*). Poor little pony. Nobody wants him. (*To* THIN.) Don't you feel any pity for the animal? Whatever's happened, you owe him the happiest moments of your childhood.

THIN. But that butler ...

FAT. What butler? (*To* MEDIUM.) You, did you see any butler?

MEDIUM. Of course not.

FAT. My dear chap, I'm afraid I have nothing more to say to you in this discussion. You are suffering from hallucinations.

MEDIUM. You're a madman!

FAT. And so, as a man who is not responsible for his actions, you would do best to put yourself under the guidance of people who know what they want. You must be eliminated from society, and the best way is for society to eat you. (*To* MEDIUM.) Would you mind laying the table?

MEDIUM. Shall I put out teaspoons?

FAT. Of course. It's a proper dinner.

(MEDIUM *lays out the teaspoons.*)

MEDIUM. One or two knives?

FAT. Two.

(MEDIUM *puts out the knives.*)

MEDIUM. Napkins?

FAT. Naturally. Everything must be just so. We are men of culture. (*During this exchange* THIN *retreats to the edge of the raft, drags one of the chairs after him and hides behind it.* MEDIUM *lays a clean white tablecloth across the middle of the raft, and carefully lays two places.* FAT *stops watching* THIN. *Instead he observes* MEDIUM, *and from time to time makes signs to him about where various things should be put. Soon the table is properly laid.* THIN *watches them, horror-struck, from behind the chair.*)

THIN (*timidly*). Excuse me ...

FAT (*paying no attention to him*). Move the cutlery a little to the right.

THIN. I think I ought to tell you ... I'm poisoned ...

FAT. The fruit bowl in the centre ...

THIN. I promise it's true. I didn't want to tell you before. I would be very bad for you.

FAT (*picks up one of the forks and looks at it*). Clean this.

THIN. I'm not trying to be difficult, I just don't want to hurt you. I like a good meal myself and I know what greed can do to a man. If I wasn't poisoned I wouldn't object, I promise. But as things are, it is clearly my duty ...

FAT. Let us begin.

MEDIUM. As you say, boss. (*Takes out of the trunk a big carving knife and a sharpening steel. Both these props must be genuine. He sharpens the knife, making an authentic, unpleasant, rhythmical sound.*)

THIN (*retreating still farther right to the very edge of the raft*). I don't say it's incurable. No, all you have to do is wait a bit, and it'll go away. A day or two's rest and I'll be depoisoned. I'll lie down here in the corner so as not to disturb you. As soon as I'm depoisoned I'll tell you. I won't make any excuses then.

> (MEDIUM *is still rhythmically sharpening the knife.* FAT *looks at the 'table' once more, inclines his head, considers it, walks up to the trunk and removes from it a vase and some flowers. He puts the flowers in the vase and the vase on the tablecloth. Then he takes a few steps to the side and observes the general effect. Only now is he satisfied.*)

THIN (*becoming less and less sure of himself*). Well, maybe two days is a bit too long. One day at the most. You know the proverb, 'What you have to eat today, eat rather tomorrow' – ha, ha, ha!

> (MEDIUM *tries the sharpness of the knife with his finger.*)

I think a few hours should be enough. One hour even.

FAT. It's time to start.

> (MEDIUM *takes a step forward in the direction of* THIN.)

THIN (*hastily*). All right, all right! I agree. Only let me give you a word of advice. For your own sake.

FAT. What about?

THIN. Gastronomic advice. Advice which is exactly to the point. Don't ... don't you think it would be better if I washed my feet.

> (MEDIUM *looks inquiringly at* FAT.)

FAT. Certainly, I never thought of that. (*To* MEDIUM.) What do you think?

MEDIUM (*doubtful*). I don't know ... He might be a bit gritty ... Maybe he ought to wash.

THIN (*quickly rolling up his trouser leg*). Yes, yes, you're quite right. Hygiene is the foundation of a healthy existence. (*Scratches his leg.*) Bacteria are invisible to the naked eye, and I can feel them itching.

FAT. Very well. Personal cleanliness never did anyone any harm. On the contrary, it ensures a long and healthy life. One second and I will find you a towel.

(THIN *sits down on the edge of the raft and dangles his legs in the sea. He washes and splashes.*)

THIN. So, you two are absolutely determined to ... to ...

FAT. I thought we had made that clear.

THIN. You mentioned something about self-sacrifice ...

FAT. Yes. I said self-sacrifice was a noble idea.

THIN (*listening intently*). Yes? Tell me more.

FAT. I don't think there's anything I can add. Self-sacrifice, the readiness to dedicate oneself ...

THIN. Yes, I know, that's all true.

FAT (*standing over him with a towel*). Do you understand now? You refused to believe me before.

THIN. I must have been very immature and inexperienced ... But now I see there's something in what you say.

FAT (*encouragingly*). You still have time to reform.

THIN. I behaved disgracefully. I rejected all your arguments.

FAT. But deep down you are not entirely cynical, judging by the noble feeling I can see beginning to emerge. Don't you think that's enough on the left one?

THIN. No, I must do between the toes. So, to get back to the subject, I must tell you that within me a new, better man is beginning to awake. Er, by the way, are your minds made up irrevocably?

FAT (*impatiently*). My dear sir!

THIN. No, no, of course they are! So what was I talking about? Aha, a new, better man. Of course it is one thing to be eaten as an ordinary human sacrifice, and something quite different to be eaten as a new, better man, who out of his own dedication ... In other words, to be eaten with one's own internal consent and noble inspiration. You promise me, do you, that everything is decided?

FAT. My word of honour.

THIN. Ha! Too bad. Well then ... What was I saying? Aha, so it

gives one a feeling of satisfaction, a sense of freedom and libera-
tion …

FAT. At last you're seeing our point of view. (*To* MEDIUM.) My
friend, would you pass me the soap?

THIN (*feverishly*). Because you mustn't think I'm a mere slave.

FAT. Rest assured, we do not think of you in this way. On the
contrary, you will go down in our stomachs – I mean in our
memories – as a hero, as a luminary of disinterested dedication.
I think the left leg's all right now, don't you?

THIN (*even more feverishly*). Of course it's all right. The right leg's
all right too. Hand me the towel and I'll come out of the water.

FAT. No, I think you ought to do the right leg a bit …

THIN. Just as you like.

FAT. I think it would be better.

THIN. Yes, I was the first man to make this great decision. I was
the first man to stand up and sacrifice myself for others …

MEDIUM (*looking at* THIN *critically*). I think you need some detergent.

FAT. No, there's nothing wrong with soap. We can wait a few
seconds longer.

THIN. Wait? When my friends are hungry! Never! (*Tries to get up,
but* FAT *holds him in the sitting position.*)

FAT. A few moments on the right leg and you're finished.

THIN. My feet seem so pointless now I've seen the light. They
might as well be dirty.

FAT (*handing him the towel*). There we are, and here's the towel.
(THIN *stands up and walks to the centre of the raft.*)

THIN. Gentlemen, I thank you. At last I have become a real man.
I have found I am a man of ideals.

FAT. Don't mention it.

THIN. I have found my self-respect. After all, what is the situation?
We are three men, and out of them I am the only one who is
saving the other two. I should like, if I may, to make a short
speech on the subject of freedom.

FAT. Is it long?

THIN. No, just a few words.

FAT. All right, go ahead.

THIN (*pulls one of the chairs over to the side of the raft and climbs on to it, in the same way as during the speeches at the beginning of the play*). Freedom – means nothing at all. It is only *true* freedom ... that means anything. Why? Because it is true, and therefore better. In which case, where are we to search for true freedom? Let us think logically. If true freedom is not the same thing as ordinary freedom, where are we to find this true freedom? The answer is simple: true freedom exists only in the place where there is no ordinary freedom.

MEDIUM. Where's the salt, boss?

FAT. Don't interrupt! Honestly, what a time to ... (*Very quietly.*) At the bottom of the trunk.

THIN. And therefore I have decided ...
    (MEDIUM *goes over to the trunk and looks inside it. Then he hurries over to* FAT.)

THIN. And therefore I have decided ... (*He repeats these words and goes on repeating them like a stuck gramophone record, only not monotonously, but interpreting them in different ways, as if he were desperately searching for what it was he wanted to say.*)

MEDIUM (*with great emotion, in a semi-whisper, but extremely clearly*). Boss, I've found that tin of baked beans and sausages.

FAT. Shhhh! Hide it this instant!

THIN. ... And therefore I have decided ...

MEDIUM. To be quite frank I'd prefer baked beans. What do you think, boss?

FAT. I don't want baked beans. And anyway ...

THIN. ... And therefore I have decided ...

MEDIUM. Anyway what?

FAT (*pointing at* THIN). Can't you see? He's happy as he is!

Charlie

Translated from the Polish *Karol*

Characters

Grandpa

Grandson

Oculist

On stage there are two chairs, a cupboard and a telephone. On the wall there is a white sheet of paper with printed lines of letters and numbers of different sizes as used in eye tests. The OCULIST, *a middle-aged man in glasses, is lying on a sofa reading a book. There is a knock at the door and the* OCULIST *rises.*

OCULIST. Come in!
> (*Enter* GRANDSON *and* GRANDPA. GRANDSON, *a man of thirty, strong and angular, comes in first, followed by* GRANDPA, *a slight little old man with a white beard. He is carrying a double-barrelled shotgun over his shoulder.*)

GRANDSON. Good morning, Doctor. May I present my grand-father?

OCULIST. Come in, please. Your grandfather? He looks remarkably young for his age.

GRANDSON. I've brought him to see you, specially.

OCULIST. Why, what's happened? A shooting accident? Some-body shot in the eye?

GRANDSON. Oh no! Grandpa hasn't started shooting yet.

OCULIST. Ah! You mean the accident will happen later. You've come as a precautionary measure.

GRANDSON. There won't be any accident. Grandpa is going to shoot, and that's the end of it.

OCULIST. Is that really necessary?

GRANDSON. Doctor, Grandpa has to shoot.

OCULIST. If he observes the safety rules of shooting, I see no reason to object. Old age has its rights.

GRANDSON. Exactly. But the problem is – glasses.

OCULIST. Trouble with his sight?

GRANDSON. Grandpa can't see very well. When he gets some glasses, he'll shoot.

OCULIST. I see, I see. You mean he's going to shoot at a target?

GRANDSON. Exactly. Look, Doctor, he's searching for one now.

(GRANDPA, *who has up to now been standing quietly, begins to search the room, yard by yard, bent double, with his face almost on the floor, like a man suffering from terrible short-sightedness.*)

OCULIST. What's he looking for?

GRANDSON (*without answering the* OCULIST). Grandpa! Calm down! He's not here.

OCULIST. Precisely, there's nobody here except us.

GRANDSON. Grandpa's very vindictive. I know him.

OCULIST. A patriot?

GRANDSON. Amongst other things. But this time it's Charlie.

OCULIST. What Charlie?

GRANDSON. We'll soon see what Charlie.

OCULIST. Is he a friend of yours?

GRANDSON. That's what we've got to find out.

OCULIST. How?

GRANDSON. Grandpa has got to get some glasses. Then he'll recognize him.

OCULIST. And when he recognizes him?

GRANDSON. Then he'll shoot him. He needs glasses first so as to recognize him and then so as to shoot him. That's why we've come to you, Doctor.

(*Meanwhile* GRANDPA *looks under the sofa and under the chairs, searches everywhere but at no time takes his shotgun off his shoulder.*)

OCULIST. Has – er – Mr Charlie done anything wrong?

GRANDSON. How are we supposed to know? Grandpa hasn't got any glasses and he can't recognize him.

OCULIST. So you don't know him at all?

GRANDSON. I've been trying to explain; we're looking for him.

OCULIST. Your grandpa doesn't know him either?

GRANDSON. Without glasses? You're joking!

OCULIST. Why do you want to meet somebody you don't know?

GRANDSON. Because we can't know him until we meet him. It's quite simple.

OCULIST. But why a man called Charlie?

GRANDSON. Do you want us to shoot the first person who comes along? Sadist! You've got to have some sort of justice.

OCULIST. In that case why shoot anybody?

GRANDSON. Doctor, you said yourself, Grandpa's got to shoot. Old age has its rights.

OCULIST. But he could shoot targets, into the air, birds, maybe ...

GRANDSON. What?

OCULIST. Birds, targets ...

GRANDSON. Who?

OCULIST. What do you mean, who?

GRANDSON. I said, who's supposed to shoot at targets?

OCULIST. Well, your grandpa.

GRANDSON (*unbelievingly*). Grandpa?

OCULIST. Yes, Grandpa.

GRANDSON. You don't know him.

OCULIST. In that case, you'd better take his gun away.

GRANDSON (*in even greater disbelief*). Whose?

OCULIST (*less definitely*). Grandpa's.

GRANDSON (*in amazement*). Grandpa's?

OCULIST. Well yes, I thought ...

GRANDSON. Did you hear, Grandpa?

GRANDPA (*for a moment interrupting his search, puts his hand to his ear*). Eh?

GRANDSON. He says, take away your gun.

GRANDPA (*taking his gun off his shoulder*). Where is he?

GRANDSON. There he is, by the chair. Shall I get him for you?

OCULIST (*hastily crossing over to the side of the stage*). Well, anyway it's your private affair; I'm not interfering.

GRANDSON. Now you're talking sense. The gun's been loaded for twenty years; it just can't go on.

OCULIST. Why can't it?

GRANDSON. Ask Grandpa. Grandpa, this chap ...

OCULIST (*interrupting*). No, no ... If it can't it can't. Of course it can't.

GRANDSON. I'll ask him why not. Grandpa, this man ...

OCULIST (*interrupting again*). No, I believe you. After all, if you've got a gun ...

GRANDSON. Exactly. You've got to shoot. Before Grandpa's day his father, my great-grandpa, used to shoot, and before him his father's father. All of them shot, all the time.

OCULIST. Hm ... yes ... In that case perhaps we can start examining your grandfather.

GRANDSON. Now you're talking. Grandpa, come on, Grandpa, a little closer.

OCULIST. Would you be so good as to take a seat.

(GRANDPA *sits down in the chair offered to him, throwing his shotgun across his shoulder.*)

GRANDSON. Now, Grandpa, listen to the doctor. Pif-paf later.

OCULIST. Perhaps we could put the gun down there for the moment.

(*Uncertainly he touches the gun.* GRANDPA *objects violently.*)

OCULIST. No? All right, all right, just as you like.

GRANDSON. Grandpa never parts with his gun. He cleans it every day. We and our family – we know what our duty is.

OCULIST (*going up to the sheet of paper with the eye-tests, points to the smallest row of signs*). Can you read this?

GRANDPA (*dreamily*). Ah! I remember my old father – he let him have it, half a pound of shot right in the middle of the belly. From sixty yards, I tell you.

OCULIST. Please try and concentrate. Now then, does reading these letters cause you any difficulty?

GRANDPA (*after long hesitation*). Ah! Maybe it wasn't quite sixty. Fifty.

GRANDSON. Later, Grandpa, later. Now you must listen to what the doctor's saying.

OCULIST. Let's try again. Can you read this?

GRANDPA. Errr, no.

OCULIST. And this?

GRANDPA. No, not a thing. Where's Charlie?

GRANDSON. Be patient, Grandpa. You must listen to the doctor, otherwise there won't be any bum-bum at Charlie.

GRANDPA. I'll show him.

OCULIST. Can you read this?

GRANDPA. Er, no.

OCULIST (*consolingly*). The situation is still not hopeless. We'll carry on testing. Can you read this?

GRANDPA. You know, I'd rather put a bullet in it.

OCULIST. Or this?

GRANDPA. Oh! Doctor you really ... No, I can't.

OCULIST. Hm. The weakness of vision is really considerable. Now let's try again. Can you read this?

GRANDPA. I haven't got my glasses.

OCULIST (*to* GRANDSON). That we shall try to remedy. May I know in what circumstances your grandpa lost his keenness of vision?

GRANDSON. Through being on guard. Grandpa was always watching to see if the enemy was walking about. And, you see, our windows are dirty.

OCULIST. Yes, that strains the eyes.

GRANDSON. More than once we've told him. If only, Grandpa, you'll put off watching until Easter the windows will be cleaned. But he was in too much of a hurry. He was on watch even in his sleep. That's the sort of man he is.

OCULIST. Let's get back to the patient. (*Pointing to the largest row of letters.*) What about this?

GRANDPA. What?

OCULIST. Can you read it?

GRANDPA. Read it?

OCULIST. Yes.

GRANDPA. No.

OCULIST. One moment. (*Pulls out from behind the sofa a roll of white paper, unrolls it and fastens it to the wall. On it one single, huge letter 'A' is printed in black ink, almost as large as a man.*) Now can you?

GRANDPA. I'm hungry.

OCULIST. Stick to the point. Can you read it now?

GRANDPA. Oh, what the hell!

OCULIST (*takes from the cupboard a box full of pairs of glasses, puts a pair on* GRANDPA. *The following questions are spoken at high speed*). And now?

GRANDPA. No.

OCULIST (*changes them for another pair*). Now?

GRANDPA. No.

OCULIST (*as above*). Now?

GRANDPA. No.

OCULIST (*as above*). Now?

GRANDPA (*chuckling*). No.

OCULIST (*as above*). Now?

GRANDPA (*chuckling even more*). No.

OCULIST (*losing his patience, takes* GRANDPA *by the back of the neck and takes him right up to the sheet with the large letter 'A'*). Now?

GRANDPA (*doubling up with laughter*). Oh dear!

OCULIST. What the devil are you laughing at?

GRANDPA. It tickles.

OCULIST (*takes off the last pair of glasses and crosses his arms. To* GRANDSON). Unfortunately, there is nothing I can do.

GRANDSON. Why?

OCULIST. This is an extraordinary case.

GRANDSON. You're taking the wrong approach. Grandpa can't read.

OCULIST. You mean he's illiterate?

GRANDSON. That's right. Any objections? You're literate, and so what? Are we afraid of you? No, it's you that's afraid of us.

OCULIST. But ... it never entered my head.

GRANDSON. What?

OCULIST. I simply wanted to find out whether ... whether reading lies among the sphere of activities practised by your progenitor and ...

GRANDSON. Doctor, you're forgetting yourself! Maybe your grandpa was a progenitor but not mine! There has never been any venereal disease in our family! We're shooting men – exclusively!

OCULIST. You're missing the point! I quite simply wanted to find out whether your grandpa reads, reads, is in the habit of reading.

GRANDSON (*with pride*). My dear sir, neither my grandpa nor I have ever read anything. Is that clear? (*Pointing to the huge letter*

'*A*'.) And you wanted to force a poor old man, and exhaust
him mentally, and give him a pain in the head, eh?

OCULIST (*explaining*). No, I was simply thinking of all our plans
for universal education.

    (*Meanwhile* GRANDPA *resumes his search.*)

GRANDSON. I've got an idea.

OCULIST. Oh, I'm sure you have.

GRANDSON. Let me see that.

OCULIST. Let you see what?

GRANDSON. Don't play the fool. (*Taking a step towards the* OCULIST.)
Give them to me.

OCULIST (*stepping back*). I don't understand.

GRANDSON. Let me see your glasses.

OCULIST (*trying to turn it all into a joke*). Ha ha ha! You're a funny
one! I remember we used to make jokes like that at school.
I remember once we put a drawing-pin under the maths
teacher's ...

GRANDSON. Stop fooling about! Take your glasses off. Come on!

OCULIST (*stiffening*). I won't put up with this sort of behaviour.
My glasses are my private property.

GRANDSON. We'll give you private property. Grandpa!

OCULIST (*terrified*). No, don't!

GRANDSON. Well?

OCULIST. There's no need to upset an old man. In his excitement
he might forget himself, get carried away. I understand that.

GRANDSON. I hope I make myself clear.

OCULIST. Maybe after all I can lend you them just for a moment.
But just for a moment. Without my glasses I am almost blind.
I can hardly see anything.

GRANDSON. All right, all right, that's unimportant. (OCULIST
takes off his glasses and hands them to GRANDSON. *He turns them
round for a moment in his hand and looks at them.*) Beautiful.

OCULIST. Zeiss lenses.

GRANDSON. Shall we try them?

OCULIST (*after taking off his glasses he becomes defenceless. His movements are uncertain. Every now and then he takes a step or two in*

some direction, but uncertainly, as if after every step he was sure he had taken the wrong direction). My glasses!

GRANDSON. Grandpa! Here! Come here!

GRANDPA *(has already resumed his search and taken his gun off his shoulder, and is holding it at the ready and peering into the corners. He gets up and, with the haste typical of an old man, trots over to his* GRANDSON*).* Where? Where is he? Is he there?

GRANDSON. Calm down, Grandpa. Let's put these glasses on.

GRANDPA. Oh, I'm getting so excited!

GRANDSON. Stand up straight, Grandpa. That's it, you put them on your ears, like the doctor. *(Stepping back a pace.)* Now, what do you say?

GRANDPA *(loses his trembling fever and becomes motionless and more important-looking. He looks about himself with deliberation and surprise).* Good! Good!

GRANDSON *(excited).* What? Good, did you say?

GRANDPA *(has found just what the* OCULIST *has lost: confidence in his movements and keenness of vision. With growing satisfaction in his voice).* Good!

OCULIST. Can you really see better?

GRANDPA *(looking at him carefully).* Who's that?

GRANDSON. That's the doctor.

GRANDPA *(without taking his eyes off the* OCULIST*).* Doctor?

OCULIST. Doctor ... of medicine.

GRANDSON. A doctor, and he didn't know how to give an old man a pair of glasses.

OCULIST *(justifying himself).* This is an extraordinary case, I could never have imagined ...

GRANDPA *(still not taking his eyes off the* OCULIST, *approaches him more closely).* Do you know, it looks to me as if ...

GRANDSON. I suppose it's just bad breeding ...

OCULIST *(nervously smoothing back his hair, adjusting his dress).* I am delighted, sir, that you have recovered your keenness of vision. Delighted.

GRANDSON. What is it, Grandpa? *(Pause.)*

GRANDPA *(takes a step backwards. All the time gazing intently at the*

OCULIST *he signs to* GRANDSON *to come nearer*). You know what I rather think?

GRANDSON (*running up*). What can you see?

OCULIST (*gets up violently from his place. Walks about the room, gesticulating nervously*). For the true man of science there is no greater joy than to witness the triumph of one's own methods. To organize the blind forces of nature, to set some harmony to the free play of the elements, such achievements produce their own true reward. May I ask you to return my glasses? I am short-sighted, and my head is beginning to ache ... Furthermore, wearing somebody else's glasses may turn out harmful for you in the long run. (*Stops walking and tries to listen in on* GRANDPA *and* GRANDSON's *conversation.*)

GRANDPA. Something tells me ... (*Whispers.*)

GRANDSON (*astounded*). Good lord! Really?

(GRANDPA *points his finger at the* OCULIST *listening in. The latter realizes he has been caught in the act and starts walking again, pretending that he is occupied in expounding his opinions.*)

OCULIST. Only in the society of today have men of science received the recognition due to them. I ask you not to forget that our power has grown immeasurably since the time of Paracelsus. We are now hacking out new paths for the human race. Please return my glasses immediately.

(GRANDPA *leans over and whispers something in* GRANDSON's *ear.*)

GRANDSON. Impossible! (GRANDPA *whispers something else.*) Are you absolutely sure?

GRANDPA. Ho, ho!

OCULIST. Who can foretell what future discoveries may transform our life, in what direction particular branches of science may extend? Thought, that property which places even an uneducated man on so infinitely higher a level than that of the beasts, lies at the root of these achievements. And at the head of this great progress of humanity, this procession marching in state through the history of nature, this crusade of reason to the land of chaos and accident, go the priests of science, go we, true leaders of an army in the service of mankind. Excuse me, I must go outside for a moment.

(*During this speech the* OCULIST *has been manœuvring himself as near as possible to the door. Meanwhile* GRANDSON *has cut him off from the way out.*)

GRANDSON. Why have you gone so pale?

(*For a moment they stand opposite each other in silence.*)

OCULIST. I've gone pale? Extraordinary.

GRANDSON. White as a sheet. Or maybe we'd better say – ha! ha! – white as a corpse!

OCULIST. Metaphorical.

GRANDSON. Could be. We're uneducated. We shoot.

OCULIST. Where's the door? I can't see properly … There's such a mist in front of my eyes. I want to go outside. You admitted I was pale.

GRANDSON. That doesn't matter to us. I'd like to ask you a few questions.

OCULIST. I am not ready for them. Anyway, what about?

GRANDSON. Who about, you mean!

OCULIST. I know nobody, I've done nothing. I don't know any addresses. I won't tell you anything.

GRANDSON. And if I ask you nicely?

OCULIST. What do you want to know?

GRANDSON. Why did you want Grandpa to shoot at targets and birds?

OCULIST. In the name of humanity and of the preservation of moral laws of coexistence among men.

GRANDSON. And why did you want to take Grandpa's gun away?

OCULIST. I thought … I thought it might become dangerous and therefore …

GRANDSON. Dangerous? Who for?

OCULIST. Whatever you say he's an old man. Very honest, I'm sure, but tired by life. Weakened sense of responsibility. Still, I could be wrong.

GRANDSON. I said, dangerous for who?

OCULIST. Well, in general, for everybody.

GRANDSON. For everybody? You look at me. Am I afraid of this danger? No, and shall I tell you why?

OCULIST. How should I know? ... Maybe, lack of imagination ...

GRANDSON. I'm not afraid because I am not ... Do you know who I'm not? Well? Oh ... Oh ... Come on!

OCULIST (*stammering*). Ch ... Ch ...

GRANDSON. Well, Cha, Cha, Char ...

OCULIST. Char ...

GRANDSON. Charlie ... lie ...

OCULIST. Charlie.

GRANDSON. You see. (*Pause.*)

OCULIST (*as if to himself*). You must be joking.

GRANDSON. No man on earth who's honest and straightforward has any objection to Grandpa shooting. Those who have clear consciences can sleep in peace. But Charlie, oh he's trembling with fear, and rightly because he knows that we shall recognize him anywhere, and especially now that Grandpa's got these glasses.

OCULIST (*hysterically*). Why won't you let me go outside? It's not democratic.

GRANDSON. So much the better. At this moment millions of simple, quiet people in the world are coming in and going out whenever they want. If it was an ordinary door, on hinges, with bolts, or a swing door, or even a bead curtain, the creak and rustle of these doors would resound uninterruptedly, freely and joyfully. Only you, you do not belong to these happy kingdoms. Is that our fault?

OCULIST. What have you got against me?

GRANDSON. You are Charlie.

OCULIST. No!

GRANDSON. Who protested when I said his gun had been loaded for twenty years and that something had to be done about it? Who wanted to force Grandpa to read?

OCULIST. Nonsense!

GRANDSON. Who didn't want to give glasses to a poor old man? You are Charlie!

OCULIST. No! I swear I'm not. (*Feverishly searching in his pockets.*)
I've got my identity card, I'll show you my identity card.

GRANDSON. Your identity card doesn't mean a thing. Grandpa
recognized you, Charlie!

OCULIST. Grandpa may be mistaken!

GRANDSON. Grandpa! Let's start!

(GRANDPA *takes off the safety-catch.*)

OCULIST. Gentlemen, wait, there must be a mistake, a tragic
misunderstanding. I do not claim that Charlie is innocent. On
the contrary, he is probably an exceptionally disgusting type,
but why me? Grandpa, take a look around. There's always time
for me. I take surgery every other day between two and six.
You've got me, gentlemen, as it were, in the bank. Meanwhile
you'd do well to have a look round; really, you would. And
all this time the real Charlie is sitting cosily somewhere, drinking his milk and laughing in your face, gentlemen, the rotten
swine! Hasn't this occurred to you?

GRANDSON. It has indeed. Perhaps you aren't the only Charlie
in the world. There may be two, or three. Grandpa, when
we've done this one, we'll carry straight on looking for the others.

OCULIST. Two? Three? Ten, a hundred, maybe they're all Charlies,
all of them, but not me. And you're wasting all this time on that
one person who is not Charlie, and meanwhile all the others
are running around, free!

GRANDSON. That's an idea, Grandpa. Who said there was only
one of them? Have you got the ammunition?

GRANDPA. Ho ho! There's enough, enough for them all.

GRANDSON (*rubbing his hands*). Fine, fine. (*Runs up to* GRANDPA
and kisses him in joy.) What a grand idea, Grandpa. We'll have
a real shooting match.

OCULIST. Yes, shoot, shoot, but not at me!

GRANDSON. I think we'll do him with buckshot first, and then
with a bullet.

GRANDPA. Good idea.

OCULIST. No, no. (*Throws himself on to the floor, runs on all fours
to the sofa and crawls under it. His voice now comes out from under*

the sofa. GRANDSON *and* GRANDPA *bend down to try and spot him there).* There's no need to bother about me. I am not against shooting at all. Shooting is very good for the lungs, it's a fine sport. Not at targets or birds or anything, a true man doesn't shoot at nonsense like that. I understand, I'm on your side. I am simply surprised that the older gentleman has only got one shotgun, and that that only has two barrels. If he had eight guns, and each one had three barrels, that would still not be excessive. It's not a question of too many, he's got to have them. Wait, listen to me!

GRANDPA (*going down on to all fours with his gun pointing under the sofa*). It's dark, damn it.

GRANDSON. Shall I move the sofa?

OCULIST. I don't want anything. I don't even want the glasses. Grandpa can keep them for himself. But I want justice, I demand it! Not me but Charlie!

GRANDPA. Light a match for me, and I'll get him.

(GRANDSON *lights a match and brings it close to the sofa. The* OCULIST's *head appears; he blows, puts out the match and vanishes again under the sofa.*)

OCULIST. Gentlemen, allow me to raise the cry, 'Hurrah for shooting!' But I cannot agree that the beautiful and noble idea of shooting should be defiled by a fatal shooting accident. Gentlemen, I'm not the one who should be shot at.

GRANDPA. It's no good, I'll shoot blind.

GRANDSON (*leaning to one side*). Aim more in the middle, Grandpa.

GRANDPA. I had him there. (*Prepares and takes aim – a pause.
The* OCULIST's *hand appears from under the sofa, waving a white handkerchief.*)

GRANDSON. That's good. It means he'll come out now.

GRANDPA. Ah, today's youth!

OCULIST (*crawls out from under the sofa and stands up in front of* GRAND-PA *and* GRANDSON). All right, I'll tell you everything.

GRANDSON. Well?

OCULIST. He's coming here.

GRANDSON. Who?

OCULIST. Charlie. The real Charlie.

GRANDPA. When? When?

OCULIST. Any moment. He should be here now.

GRANDPA. Shall I shoot?

GRANDSON. In a minute, Grandpa. (*To the* OCULIST.) How can you prove to us that the man that's coming is a greater Charlie than you?

OCULIST. Because of various things he said about you.

GRANDSON. What things?

OCULIST. Various things.

GRANDSON. What does that mean?

OCULIST. Shall I repeat them?

GRANDSON. Yes.

OCULIST. He said that you are murderers.

GRANDSON. Oh, he said that, and what else?

OCULIST. That your grandpa is a blood-sucking old idiot ...

GRANDSON. What?

OCULIST. I'm just repeating what I heard. As for you, he said you're an unbelievable fool and a pervert and a typical product of your nauseating family. Shall I go on?

GRANDSON. Everything.

OCULIST. He said that the very fact of your existence is sufficient proof of the senselessness and rottenness of the world, to such an extent that to be murdered, even by you, would be a merciful relief, and a splendid way of ceasing to share with you what is common to humanity.

GRANDSON. Did you hear that, Grandpa?

GRANDPA. Charlie! As if I heard his very words! That's Charlie.

GRANDSON. And what else?

OCULIST. And he also said, I don't know whether it's true, that you ... I can't say it ...

GRANDSON. I tell you, don't conceal anything.

OCULIST. No, I really can't.

GRANDSON. Tell me at once!

OCULIST. He said that you belch. (*Pause.*)

GRANDSON. The swine! Why didn't you tell me this before?

OCULIST. Because I've only just realized. I must admit that before you came here the idea of Charlie was quite new to me. But this discussion has opened my eyes. I am not Charlie; you don't believe me – too bad. But I cannot bear the idea that I will die and that the real Charlie will be walking about and laughing in your face. For what guarantee have I that, having once made a mistake about me and taken me for Charlie, you won't in turn make a mistake about Charlie and take him for me, for an innocent person. It's not so much a question of my life as of justice. You said yourself that there must be some justice, that one can't just shoot at anybody in the street. So, when I was lying under the sofa I thought to myself: my God, how tragic that these two gentlemen, instead of just resting, are spending their time chasing this Charlie, little knowing that their efforts will be quite wasted. So, I decided to rebel, I rejected the rest of my former pseudo-morality and resolved to tell all.

GRANDSON. Listen. The fact that you're Charlie is another matter. Grandpa recognized you, and he doesn't make mistakes. But it's true that there may be more than one Charlie. We shall wait here. If he doesn't come, we'll do you in and go. If he does come, we'll do him in and then think about it. It's quite possible that you know the whole organization. Why is he coming here, anyway?

OCULIST. He's my patient. Like you.

GRANDSON. Let's ambush him, Grandpa.

(GRANDSON *puts the chair opposite the door.* GRANDPA *kneels behind the chair with the gun pointing at the door.* GRANDSON *stands well back in the stage behind the cupboard.* OCULIST, *completely exhausted, sits on the sofa and wipes his forehead with a handkerchief. He covers his face with his hands.* GRANDPA *and* GRANDSON, *having taken up their positions, begin to wait. The stage grows slightly darker.*)

GRANDSON. I can't see him.

OCULIST. He's not a young man. He walks slowly.

(*Pause. Silence.*)

GRANDSON. He ought to be here now.

OCULIST. He'll come. He's sure to come. He's always punctual, and so well-mannered.
   (*Pause. Silence.*)
GRANDSON. There's something I don't like about this.
OCULIST. Why? The weather's nice ... a beautiful sunset.
GRANDPA. I'm bored.
OCULIST. Shall I read something? (*Without waiting for an answer he opens a book and reads, holding it very close to his eyes.*) ' ... the traveller who attains the valley from the direction of the south-east will be greeted by a most impressive landscape. The vine-covered slopes promise that not only the marvellous vistas, purity of the air and colourfulness of the different flowers comprise the feast with which the surrounding district regales the newcomer. In truth, both spiritual and other advantages await in abundance all those who do not recoil before what is good and beautiful. The local inhabitants, though generally of moderate height, are attractively built ... '
GRANDSON. Enough!
OCULIST. Just as you say. (*Closes the book.*)
GRANDSON. How much longer do we wait?
OCULIST. The whole fun of the hunt is waiting. (*Changing the subject.*) Shall I make you some coffee?
GRANDSON. No need. We don't drink coffee.
   (*Pause. Silence.* OCULIST *remains motionless. Suddenly he gets up again and begins to creep about the room. It continues to get just perceptibly darker.*)
GRANDSON. What is it?
OCULIST. A fly. (OCULIST *performs the usual waves of the hand, closing his fist, preceded by a quiet creeping noise. The fly keeps getting away.*)
GRANDSON (*with interest*). Got it?
OCULIST. Missed it. Ah, there it is!
   (*Pause.* GRANDPA *stops looking at the door; in spite of himself he is drawn into the fly-hunt.*)
GRANDSON. Now! Left hand!
   (*A longer pause in which the* OCULIST *carries on his pantomime.*

He is enthralled, rapt, his mind completely concentrated on the chase. He alternately creeps along and then hurls himself forward. Being deprived of his glasses he guides himself more by ear. At a certain moment the fly settles on the gun of GRANDPA who has been kneeling down all this time and following the hunt simply by the motion of his head. GRANDSON, leaning out from behind the cupboard, watches the scene intently. OCULIST approaches the gun, and hovers menacingly over it. This is the moment of sharpest tension. Then suddenly he performs a lightning sweep of the hand along the barrel and stays motionless with closed fist. · He looks first at GRANDPA and then at GRANDSON then very slowly opens his hand.)

OCULIST. Missed!

(Footsteps are heard on the other side of the door coming nearer and nearer. It is getting darker and darker.)

GRANDSON *(exclaims triumphantly)*. He's coming!

GRANDPA *(lets out something that resembles a joyful yodelling noise)*. Halla – lii ... !

(OCULIST throws himself desperately on to the sofa and covers his head with a cushion.)

GRANDSON *(blissfully)*. Now's your chance!

GRANDPA. Like my father!

GRANDSON. And your grandfather!

GRANDPA. Forward! Charge! *(A knock at the door. GRANDPA questioningly to GRANDSON.)* Now?

GRANDSON. Just a minute. *(Draws from his bosom a bugle and plays a few notes of a rousing song. Renewed knocking.)* Now!

(The door opens slowly. GRANDPA fires both barrels. Silence.)

GRANDSON *(runs out from the corner behind the cupboard and gazes at the door which is still open)*. Got him!

GRANDPA *(slowly puts down his gun and stretches his limbs)*. Well, that's a relief.

GRANDSON *(yawning)*. A tense moment.

GRANDPA *(pointing at the OCULIST who is still lying motionless covered with a cushion)*. And what about him?

OCULIST. My glasses!

GRANDPA. That's a great load off my mind.

GRANDSON. You see, Grandpa, the world is not so wicked.

OCULIST (*slowly sitting up on the sofa*). Is it all over?

GRANDSON (*clapping him on the shoulder*). It looks like you were telling the truth. He's lying there, on the floor.

OCULIST (*lethargically*). Yes, yes ... And how is Grandpa feeling now?

GRANDSON. Grandpa? Grandpa has never felt better in his life. You've cured him, Doctor. Charlie was what he needed.

OCULIST (*all the time as in a dream*). I am very happy, very happy.

GRANDSON. And we must be off now. Grandpa has got to load both barrels.

OCULIST. Again?

GRANDSON. Then we'll be back. (*Pause.*)

OCULIST. Then ... then you're going to go to all this trouble again.

GRANDSON. I'm afraid so. It could be that some Charlie is going to come here again, and even if he doesn't ...

OCULIST. But I thought ...

GRANDSON. You thought we weren't coming back, did you? Well, you needn't worry. There's enough ammunition. He's got his glasses. All he needs is his good health.

OCULIST. So when can I expect you?

GRANDSON (*threatening him jokingly with his finger*). Eh, eh! Don't you be so curious. We could be here tomorrow, in two days or maybe in ten minutes. Any time's a good time to shoot Charlie, as our saying goes.

OCULIST (*resignedly sitting on the sofa with his head in his hands*). So I'll have to ...

GRANDSON. Come on, Grandpa. Slope arms and forward march. How much do we owe you?

OCULIST. Oh, nothing. We'll put it down to national insurance.

GRANDSON (*giving him his card*). This is our telephone number. If ever anything ...

GRANDPA. Straight between the eyes, my friend. And remember an old man's advice: tea should be hot, an 'i' should have a dot, and Charlie should be ...

GRANDSON (*impatiently*). Come on, Grandpa, let's go. (*They leave the room.* GRANDSON *lets* GRANDPA *pass through and moves back from the door towards the* OCULIST.) And if you know anybody else ...

OCULIST. Yes? (*Pause. They look at each other.*)

GRANDSON. Because we'll be back. (*Leaves the room. He stops in the doorway and says to himself, looking down at what is lying on the floor outside –*)

GRANDSON. So he said I belch ... (*Really goes out this time.*)

> (*The* OCULIST *sits still for some time as before. It has got much darker but now stops darkening. Then he gets up slowly, goes out and drags into the room an inert figure. It is a dummy, of course. The corpse is not played by a live actor. He places the dummy on the sofa, lays its hands on its chest, then examines its eyes, turns back the eyelids and looks at the eyes according to the rules of eye-tests.*)

OCULIST. Incurable separation of the cornea. Of course, the shock of the blast may have hastened the onset of the disease, but who can guarantee that tomorrow he wouldn't have fallen down the stairs, and then his cornea would have become separated completely? In any case there was nothing I could do for him. (*Pause.*) He didn't have to come either. His appointment wasn't for today. I was taking a chance. (*Pause.*) I'm shortsighted too and I'm still alive. (*The telephone rings. The* OCULIST *lifts the receiver.*) Hello! ... Yes, can I help you? ... Yes, speaking ... Between two and six ... Whenever it's convenient ... Four o'clock? All right, tomorrow at four. Don't you worry, we'll soon fix you up. Can I have your name? (*Pulls a notebook and pencil out of his pocket. Begins to write.*) I must write it down in the appointments book ... Hello! Yes. Now then ... name – Charlie. Till tomorrow then. Goodbye. (*Replaces the receiver. Walks away from the telephone, looks at his watch, glances at the door, listens through the keyhole, then suddenly opens the door to check that nobody's listening. Reflects for a moment. Suddenly he runs to the telephone and hurriedly dials a number.*) Hello, hello! Who's speaking? Grandpa? Grandpa, this is the doctor. Yes,

the doctor. What do you mean, what doctor? (*Ingratiatingly.*)
Don't you recognize my voice? Don't you recognize your own
doctor? ... Well then, Grandpa, tomorrow at four. Yes, tomorrow at four. He'll be here. Who? What do you mean who?
Charlie, of course. Well, cheerio! Till tomorrow! Goodbye!
(*Pause. The* OCULIST *replaces the receiver, walks up to the sofa,
lifts the dummy off it and pushes it underneath. He himself lies down
on the sofa, opens his book and begins to read it just like at the beginning
of the play.*)

The Party

Translated from the Polish *Zabawa*

Characters

Farmer B

Farmer S

Farmer N

The term 'farmer' does not mean the men should be portrayed as 'village types', nor do they speak with a regional accent.

Stage completely dark. Voices.

VOICE B. What's going on?

VOICE N. It's locked.

VOICE S. Maybe they're out.

B. What do you mean locked?

N. Hey! Hello, hello!

S. It's us!

B. What do you mean, out?

N. Let us in!

S. They're happier on their own.

B. What do you mean, happier on their own?

N. Open the door!

S. If they weren't happier on their own, they'd let us in.

B. Let's see.

   (*Loud knocking. Pause.*)

N. Maybe they can't hear?

B. What do you mean, can't hear? (*Loud knocking.*) Hey, you! Open the door!

S. Where's the doorman?

N. Give it a kick.

   (*Even louder knocking. A moment's break.*)

S. Not a sound.

N. Try again.

B. Sh! Quiet!

N. Why sh? There's a party going on.

B. Sh! Let's listen.

N. Well?

B. I can hear people. There's something rustling, something walking about.

S. They don't want us!

B. They don't want us?

N. Us?

S. They don't want us.

B. They don't want us at the party?

S. No. They don't.

B. Let's go in!

N. But it's locked!

B. Hold my jacket.

S. Let me get at it.

B. All right! O-o-o-ne!

(*Noise of a body hitting the door.*)

N. Done it?

B. No, I'll try again! O-o-o-ne!

(*Noise.*)

N. Well?

S. Well?

B. All together now!

B, S AND N (*in chorus*). A-a-a one! A-a-a one! A-aa—

(*A triple bang, then a piercing crash, and suddenly a bright light is turned on. On the stage is a table, large enough for ten or even twenty people, of dark, good-quality wood. It is bare, without a tablecloth. On the ceiling is a garland made of dusty tissue-paper, like in provincial club halls. There is a large bulging cupboard and lots of stools, easy chairs, hard-backs and other types, old and worn-out. All of them, like the table, are stylishly made, but they are strewn untidily around the room. A double-bass in a black case is leaning against the wall; on the floor is a concertina. There is nothing on the table except a quarter-litre bottle of vodka. It is made of white glass and is unopened. The walls have been delicately tattooed by time and there are no pictures. The only decorations are garlands of cheap faded tissue-paper and one brown hanging drapery. There are no windows. Right in the middle of the front wall, in a heavy, dark, decorative recess, is a huge high door, now partly smashed, with splinters of wood hanging from it. It is dark on the other side of the opening. The three* FARMERS *tumble through this door on to the stage. They are wearing black Sunday suits, and each man has a brightly coloured flower in his buttonhole.* FARMER B, *who is hefty and tall with a fresh complexion, is putting on his jacket as he runs. There is a dark-blue scarf round his neck; the others are wearing ties. They are all young and have thick untidy hair: B's is black, N's fair, and S's red. They are actually wigs, but are not exaggerated or caricatured. They charge madly about the stage.*)

B. Yoo-hoo! Music! Music!

N. We thought you didn't want us.

B. We're here, we're here! Music!

S (*looking round*). There's nobody here!

B. There must be! (*To* N.) You're there. I'm here.

   (B *and* N *run off to opposite corners, searching.* S *glances about.*)

N. Not a soul.

B. What do you mean, not a soul?

S. If there was anyone, they'd be here.

B. There's the concertina, but where are the people?

S. A concertina, but no music.

B. So what's missing?

S. What isn't missing?

B. Sit down!

   (*He sits down.*)

N. I'm not going to sit down. Orchestra! Where are you? (*Begins to sob.*)

B. What's wrong with him?

S. Crying ... is he?

N (*sobbing*). There was going to be a party ...

B. Be quiet!

N (*with some effort takes off a shoe and shows it to the others*). I bought ... these shoes ...

S. Control yourself.

N. These new shoes ... I bought them ... Now what am I going to do?

S. Perhaps they'll come back.

B. They haven't gone anywhere. They're here. I can feel it. Be quiet and put your shoe on.

(N *meekly puts his shoe back on, still sobbing a little.*)

s. What do you mean, they're here? Can you see them?

b. If they weren't here, they'd have let us in. They didn't want to let us in, so they must be here.

n. That's right!

s. Either they're here or they're not.

b. And we won't go without a party.

n. If they're here, there must be a party.

s. If there's a party for them, there's a party for us. But where is it?

n. Where is this party?

b. I told you to be quiet. There *is* a party, because they're here.

n. Where?

b. Here.

n. Then why can't we see them?

b. They've got to play the music: that concertina and that double-bass.

    (N *suddenly begins to sing a well-known tune. He completes one four-line verse.*)

s. And what if they don't play?

b. They've got to play; there's a party. O.K.?

    (N *sings one line of the same song.*)

b. Shhh! We won't sing till they play the music.

    (N *sits down comfortably in an armchair, putting his feet on the table.*)

s. I think ...

b. Don't think.

s. I think they've got something against us.

b. I said don't think!

s. It's my brain thinking. Why is it all so quiet?

b. You watch out!

n. (*suddenly*). Why isn't there any party for us?

b. Why is it so quiet?

s. Why aren't they playing music?

b. They're not playing because they're going to play. If they were playing they couldn't be going to play.

s. That's not the reason. I tell you: they think we're worse.

b. Worse?

s. That's what they think.

b. There he goes!

(*S and B run about looking for the enemy.*)

s (*straining his eyes*). There's nobody.

b. Let's smash it!

s. What?

b. All this!

(*They overturn several of the chairs. B gets hold of the concertina, lifts it up and hurls it against the wall with a crash. S does exactly the same thing. B makes as if to do it again and bends down, but N, in his protest-demonstration, wanders round the stage, comes upon him, thrusts his shoe under B's nose, and interrupts him.*)

b. What do you want?

n. Nothing. But I bought a shoe.

b. Get out of the way.

n. (*goes away, sits down, puts the shoe on, looks at it with interest and repeats appreciatvely*). A new one.

(*B and S simultaneously take out combs and carefully comb their hair.*)

b. Three! Four!

b, s and n (*all standing to attention, together in a chorus, very loudly*). We are not worse!

s. I've had another thought ...

b. You keep quiet, keep quiet!

s. If we're not worse, maybe they're better?

b. They're better?

s. Because if we're not worse, maybe they're better.

n (*trying to pull his shoe off again*). This shoe ... I ... This shoe ... I ...

b (*lifting up a chair and threatening him with it*). Put your shoe on!

s. Otherwise what can it be? Why is there no party?

(*Meanwhile N, not allowed to protest with his shoe, gets up and quietly throws the concertina against the wall.*)

b. Don't interrupt!

N (*sadly*). Are they better ... ?

B (*sternly*). We're better too!

S. Where's the party?

B. I tell you, we're better too.

S. But there's no party.

B. There's going to be, there must be a party!

N. Oh, if there's going to be, that's a different matter. (*Walks away from the concertina, pacified.*)

S (*hopefully*). Will there really?

B (*as if giving a military order*). Sii–iit down. (*Pause.*) They're worse! (*Pause.*) They're worse too.

S. What did you say?

B. I said even if they're better, we're better too. Just as better.

S. I didn't say anything.

B. But what were you thinking?

S. I wasn't thinking anything.

B. Then why not say something? (*Pause.*)

S. The thing is they're not here. If they were here we could get to grips with them.

B. They *are* here!

S. Where?

B. Here.

N. They're not.

B. Shhh!

S. The table's not laid.

B. Shh! Quiet! They *are* here. There must be something. (*Pause.*)

N (*suddenly jumps up*). Yes!

B. What?

S. What are you looking at?

N (*points to the table*). Yes! There *is*! There's a *party*!

B. Didn't I tell you?

S. There's a party!

N. Hurrah! Yoo-hoooo!

B. Three! Four!

(B, S *and* N *sing together in chorus the same four-line verse that* N *sang a few moments ago.*)

B. Rah-diddle-diddle-om-pom! Hurrah!

S. Yoo-hoooo!

(*S and B launch themselves into a country dance. N pounds his fist on the table, imitating a drum, and sings at the top of his voice another four-line verse of a folk song.*)

Yoo-hoo-hoo!

(*S and B begin to dance more slowly as they gradually realize that nothing is happening, and soon the country dance withers away. N too gets thrown off his stride, beats time less often and less certainly; finally he stops completely. Silence. S and B look at each other.*)

B (*to S.*) Did you hear anything?

S. No. There wasn't any music. What about you?

B. Not a thing.

S (*pointing to N*). It was him.

B (*to N*). What did you say about a party?

N. Well, there's this, isn't there? (*Lifts the bottle off the table.*)

S. What about the party?

N. If they put this on the table, it means there must be a party.

B. A quarter of a bottle?

N. They've put it ready for a wedding feast. My daddy told me about wedding feasts. You get a table, a big one for a big wedding feast and a small one for a little wedding feast. And when you've got the table, you lay out the stuff on top. 'Remember, my son,' Daddy used to say, 'when you see a table and something on the table, it means the wedding feast is going to start.'

B. A quarter of a bottle? Chuck it away.

N (*clumsily raising his fist at B*). Are you insulting my father?

B. Chuck it out!

N. We'll knock the cork out. (*Tries to knock out the cork.*)

B (*twists N's arm and takes the bottle away from him*). So this is your wedding party? This? (*Walks round the table striking it with his hand at regular intervals.*) We'll count it up. First, I don't give a damn for your father. Second, where's the toast-master? Three, the best man? Four, the pork chops? Five and six, the bride? Where's the lemonade? Where are the sausages? Seven, eight!

The salads, the stews and the soups? Nine, ten! And the bride-groom?

N. He hasn't arrived yet.

S. And where's the beer?

B. Yes! Where's the beer?

N. I suppose they're pouring it out.

S. You'd have to do a penance for laying a table like this.

B. Eleven! (*Seizing N by his lapels and shaking him.*) The music! Where's the music?

N. Somewhere around.

B. You call this a party? A *party*?

S. With no music? What about the dancing?

N. There isn't any.

S. Idiot!

B (*letting N go*). Twelve! This table – it's chronic! My God, you think a quarter of a bottle …

N. It's never very much. Daddy says …

B. Either the party's here or it isn't. Nuts to your daddy. You get a quarter of a bottle and you think that's enough. You'd have fallen for that old trick! (*Raises his arm as if to smash the bottle against the wall. S skilfully slips the bottle out of his hand and puts it away under the table. To N, scornfully.*) And you'd have fallen for it!

N. When they put a …

B. Why do you think we came here, you clown?

N. I thought, if you've got a table, and there's a …

S. They put bottles out for funerals.

B (*staggered*). You're right.

    (B, S *and* N *look at each other, quite taken aback.*)

S (*lowering his voice*). We'd better find out.

B (*persuasively, but lowering his voice also*). But we were asked to a party …

S. So what? People do have funerals.

N. Funerals?

S. And if it's not a wedding feast …

N. My God!

B (*loudly*). We were asked to a party ... !

S. Shhh ...

B (*whispering*). If we were asked to a party ... why did they .. ? (*Loudly.*) Aaaah, nonsense.

N. A funeral!

B. There'd be people in mourning.

S (*points to the double-bass in its case*). That's black.

B (*uncertainly*). That's the orchestra.

S. It was all quiet when we came.

B. There were people. We listened at the door.

S. So what? It could have been a funeral.

N. People come to funerals.

B. I tell you, it's a party.

N. And what if they're here?

B. They aren't here.

N. They are here. You said so yourself.

B. But they've gone.

N. When are they coming back?

B. They aren't coming back.

S. But you said they're here. Don't deny it.

B. They aren't.

N. Well, that means it's a funeral. If it was going to be a party you'd have said they're here. (*Takes the flower out of his buttonhole and puts it away in his pocket.*)

S. We'd better kneel down.

B. I'm not kneeling.

S. If we want to find out ...

B. There'd be people in mourning.

N. Shall I kneel?

B. Stand up!

S. There's something on the floor! (*Picks up a long, black wig from the floor among the piles of chairs.*)

N. It's hair!

S. Black hair.

B. Show me!

N. It's black!

B. What about it? (S *and* N *stare at* B.) What are you looking at?

S. Your hair ...

B. It's not mine!

N. It's your hair!

B. What do you mean, my hair? (*Upset.*) Do you want a punch on the nose?

N. Good lord!

B. Where's the funeral? What are you looking at?

S. Your hair's black.

B. It's not!

N. He wears that on his head! Christ!

S. Do you want a mirror?

B. No I don't.

S (*offering him the wig*). Try it on.

B (*stepping back violently*). I don't want to.

S. It's the same.

B. Throw it away!

S. Isn't it yours?

B. I said throw it away!

N. They're coming back! They're coming back!

S (*puts the wig on his own head. Thoughtfully inspects his sleeves and trouser legs.*) It's just ... black clothes.

B. Take it off!

S (*running towards him*). Who's blacker? (B *runs away from him round the table.*) Let's see who's blacker.

B. No.
  (*The double-bass in the black case, which has been lying against the wall, suddenly falls over, probably as a result of the floor shaking as they run. S and B stand motionless.*)

N (*drops on to his knees*). They're here! They're here!

B. I said stop that.
  (S, *gazing at the double-bass, slowly takes off his wig and puts it on the table. He takes the flower out of his buttonhole and puts it away in his pocket. Kneels down next to N.*)

N. I think I'll kneel down too.

B. I'm not kneeling.

s. It's the custom.

b. You can't be sure.

s. We should have come earlier.

b. They wouldn't have let us in.

n. Shall I pray for eternal requiem?

s. No, wait. We don't know what's happening yet.

b *(removes his blue scarf and puts it in his pocket)*. You make me laugh. *(S and N pay no attention to him.)* You're like sheep!

n. I'm praying in my thoughts.

s. Leave me alone.

n. I'm praying.

b. It can't be a funeral ... They'd have rung the bells! *(S and N pay no attention to him. B takes the scarf out of his pocket, lays it carefully on the floor and somewhat unwillingly goes down on to one knee.)* It can't be a ... *(S and N remain silent.)* My shoe-lace is undone ... *(Pause.)*

n. I've finished praying.

s. Don't interrupt.

n. Amen. *(Pause.)*

b. Hey!

s. Yes, what is it?

b. If it's a funeral, why have they got this concertina and this double-bass?

n. Exactly!

b. What are these decorations for? *(Gets up.)*

n. He's right.

b. It's not a funeral party.

n *(still kneeling)*. Shall we sing a hymn?

s *(gets up)*. Maybe there's no funeral party, but we still haven't found the wedding party.

b. There is one, though.

n. Why haven't we found it?

b *(pointing to S)*. He'll tell you.

s. Why me?

b *(confidentially)*. What was that idea of yours?

s. I'm not sure about it.

B. Tell us, anyway.

S. Maybe they've got something against us.

B. What could they have against me?

S. Nothing.

B. Or against you?

S. How should I know?

B. Have you done anything to them?

S. No.

(B *surreptitiously takes the black drapery and throws it over* N, *who is still kneeling down. He covers him with the cloth, topples him over and winds it round him.* N *defends himself desperately, but* B *is stronger and has the advantage of having taken him by surprise. After a moment he sits on* N, *who is wound up in the cloth and struggling helplessly, emitting inarticulate cries from inside the package.*)
What ... What ... What are you doing?

B. It's him.

S. Let him go!

B. I won't let him go. It's him!

S. What do you mean, it's him, you great cow?

B. I'm not a cow!

S. Let him go!

B (*in a stubborn, solemn and injured tone*). I'm not a cow.

S (*withdrawing*). All right, you're not. But what are you doing to him?

B. He's guilty.

S (*seizing a chair and running towards* N *who is still wound up in the drapery*). Hold him down!

B. He's still struggling! What are you struggling for, you great cow? He's guilty.

N (*indistinctly, from inside the drapery*). I'm not a cow!

S (*checking the impetus of his run*). What's he guilty of?

B. It's his fault there's no party.

S. Why?

B. They've got something against him.

S. Why him?

B. Is it you, then?

s. Certainly not.

b. Have you done anything to them?

s. No.

b. Nor have I. They've got nothing against me either. That means they must have something against him, or else they'd be playing the music. He's worse.

s. It looks like it.

b. There'll be a party now.

s. What if there isn't?

b. Just wait a minute. There'll be one now. Listen!

s. What?

b. Music! (*S listens. B repeats impatiently.*) Was that music?

s. No.

b. Listen properly.

s. I can't hear anything.

b. Listen more carefully.

s. There's no music.

b. What do you mean?

s. All right, you listen. I'll hold him. (*They change places. S sits on N, B gets up and listens.*) Can you hear music?

b. Wait. (*Walks round the stage, listens. He is clearly surprised.*) There isn't any.

s. Shall I let him go?

b. It's incredible ... (*Stands there thoughtfully, his back towards S and N, staring at the instruments. N, who has now been released, springs to his feet and kicks B in the pants. B turns round and says sadly.*) There's no music.

   (*N wants to kick B again, but he remembers that he has new shoes on. He stops, spits on a shoe and wipes it with his sleeve.*)

s (*ironically*). Very clever!

b. I don't understand.

n. You pigs!

s. Listen.

b. Why on earth ... ?

s. Perhaps there isn't meant to be a party?

b. What?

N. No party?

S. If there's no party, perhaps there isn't meant to be one?

B. For us?

S. Not for us. For everyone. There's just no party.

B. None at all?

S. It doesn't exist.

N. Nonsense!

B. How can there be no party when there *may be* a party? That means there is one.

S. Prove there's going to be a party.

B. And you prove there isn't going to be a party.

N. Prove it!

S. Where did you get the idea of a party?

B. If it's an idea, it must mean something: it means maybe there's a party.

S. There's no maybe about it. There can't be one, because there isn't one.

B. But there must be.

N. Oh!

S. Why must there?

B. Because I want one.

S. You really want one?

B. You think I don't want one?

N. Tell him you want one.

B. Of course I want one.

S. How do you know you want one?

B. Because I know I want one. I feel like one.

N. Quite right!

S. But there isn't one.

B. That's bad.

S. Why is it bad? If there was going to be one, and there wasn't one, that would be bad.

B. I still think it's bad. There must be a party.

N. Yes.

S. If there's no party, there isn't going to be one, there mustn't be one.

B. Why mustn't there be one? I like it when there's a party.

S. Well, so what? You like it and so what? Does that mean there's going to be one?

B. There must be!

N. Yes! There must be!

S. Who said so?

B. I did!

S. *They* didn't, though.

B. But I did.

S. We ought to have stayed at home. We go out looking for them, we leave home, we walk all the way there, we look around and not a soul. It's terrible.

B. Terrible for me.

S. Listen! Were you going to the party, or was the party coming to you?

B AND N (*together*). We're going to the party!

S. Aha! We're going to the party. That means it's somewhere away from home, and if it's away from home, it must be written down somewhere where it's taking place. Because if it's not written down ...

N. They don't have parties at home. Only once. I remember, a fly flew into my daddy's soup. My daddy's short-sighted and he ate it. It was marvellous. (*Sadly.*) But they didn't have an orchestra.

S. You show me where it's written down, in what book. Where did they write it down?

B. I'll show you!

S. Right!

N (*looking around*). There aren't any books here.

B. Maybe there are some in the cupboard. (*To* S.) Well?

S. O.K. We'll try it.

B. Want to bet?

S. Certainly.

B. How much?

S. The one who loses has to leave the room.

B. And not come back?

s. And not come back. (*Seeing that* B *is hesitating.*) Are you afraid?

b. Afraid?

s. If you lose, it means there's no party. Why stay if there's nothing for you to do?

b. I agree. (*They shake hands.*) Shall I look?

s. I'm waiting.

> (B *opens one door of the cupboard. In the dark interior they see the long white shape of a cadaverous skull.* B *slams the door violently and leans against it with his back.*)

n. Ah! (*Falls to his knees.*)

b (*in a whisper*). Did you see?

s (*in a whisper*). Was it a real one?

b. Large as life.

n (*backing away from the cupboard on his knees*). I don't believe it!

b. You want another look?

n. Stop him!

s. Now I understand.

b. Oh do you?

s. You've lost.

b. I've lost?

s. You showed me yourself.

b. It's not in writing.

s. That doesn't matter.

b. There's nothing written down.

s. So you admit you've lost!

b. I haven't lost.

s. Where's your evidence?

b (*threateningly*). I'll give him a good ...

s (*sneeringly*). That's not very polite.

b. Shall I hit him?

n. No, stop it.

s. Get out of here. You've lost.

b. I'm not going.

s. What does it matter to you? There's no wedding party.

b. There's going to be one, because there must be one. I'm not going.

s. And that thing in the cupboard?

B. There's no coffin, so there's no funeral. It's a party.

s. Where's your proof?

B. All in good time.

s (*turning to* N). He's still hoping, because he doesn't want to go away. (*To* B.) You're still hoping, aren't you?

B. I know for certain.

s. Show me in writing.

B (*violently*). I'm going to hit him.

N. Leave him alone.

(B *opens wide one door of the cupboard and stands to one side of it, as if inviting the apparition to emerge.* N *covers his eyes with his hands.* S *retreats discreetly. Pause.*)

B (*seeing that nothing is happening, looks into the cupboard and shouts triumphantly*). It's not real.

(B *pulls out of the cupboard a mask known popularly as a 'death mask'; but it is different from those sold in shops in that it is very carefully constructed, and not grey but blindingly white, for which reason the audience was able to see it in the dark interior of the cupboard.*)

N (*gets up from his knees*). I thought it was another funeral.

B (*putting the mask on, to* S). Were you frightened?

s. It's a swindle.

B (*triumphantly*). I haven't lost! Do you believe me now? (*Takes off the mask and gives it to* S.)

s (*putting on the mask*). It doesn't make any difference. There's no proof.

N. What's it for?

B. There's a whole theatre here!

(B *takes out of the cupboard two more masks: one of a king wearing a crown, with a rough bricky surface, and another of a delicately beautiful woman, rather like a Virgin Mary in medieval sculptures, but quite bald. The masks are larger than life and the mouths are left uncovered, so as not to hinder the wearer's speech.*)

N. I want to be the king!

(B *gives* N *the king's mask. He puts it on.*)

B (*putting on the woman's mask and rubbing his hands*). O.K., boys, who's for beer? We'll have a Christmas play and some dancing.

N. What about the music?

S. It's Christmas Eve, not a wedding night.

B. There are bridesmaids, though. Look what I've found! (*Pulls out of the cupboard three women's hats and three pairs of shoes with very high heels.*)

N (*enthusiastically*). This is marvellous!

B (*to* S). What have you got to say?

S. It should all be written down.

N. I'm enjoying myself!

B (*triumphantly*). What's this?

(*He takes out a white garment, which turns out to be a woman's dress, waves it around in the air and throws it. In the same way he removes from the cupboard two more dresses, both of them bright and garish, one of them cherry coloured. All the dresses are in contemporary style, not fancy costumes.*)

N (*pleasantly surprised*). They must have stripped naked!

S (*stubbornly*). I still want it in writing.

B. Isn't this enough for you?

N. Where are the girls?

S. It all ought to be in a book.

N. Tell them to come out!

B. Aha! You want a book! Here's a book. (*Takes a book out of the cupboard.*)

S. Now we'll find out for sure.

N (*taking off his king's mask and putting it on the table*). Girls, girls, the boys are here!

B (*lifting up the book*). It's all down here. Everything will be explained. Soon the party will begin.

(N *transfers the flower from his pocket to his buttonhole.*)

B. Out you come, ladies!

(*During the next sequence* S *and* B *in their excitement do not take off their masks.*)

S. O.K. This is what my bet's about.

B. Let's read it.

N (*knocking on the closed door of the cupboard*). Stop flirting.

S. This was your idea. I warn you.

B. It was your idea too. Do you want to back out?

S. It's you who's backing out.

B. No! We made a bet.

N (*to the cupboard*). I'll look inside.

S. I warned you!

> (B *and* S *walk briskly up to the table.* B *throws the book on to the centre of the table.*)

N (*coquettishly*). The first one I see belongs to me.

S. Let's begin!

> (S *and* B *take up positions at opposite ends of the table.* N *looks behind the closed door of the cupboard, stoops and inserts the whole upper half of his body inside it.*)

B. Well?

S. Well what?

B. Read it!

S. Me?

B. You still won't believe me.

N. (*returns carrying three brassières*). They've gone.

S. Don't interrupt.

N. It's a hard life for an honest man. (*Downhearted, sits down away from the others.*)

B. Are you going to read?

S (*uncertainly*). What, this?

B. You suggested it.

S. You agreed with me.

N (*picks up the cherry-coloured dress, looks down into it through the décolletage, like into a sack, puts one hand in, then the other, then puts his whole head in*). Absolutely nothing.

B (*pointing to* N). Let him read it.

N. Me read it?

> (B *and* S *run up to him on either side, take him by the arms and seat him at the table, in the middle facing the audience.*)

B (*opening the book in front of him at the title page*). Read it!

S. Begin at the beginning.

B. Don't leave anything out.

N (*hums and hahs*). I've got a frog in my throat.

B. It'll be better when you start reading.

N. What shall I read about?

B. Is there going to be a party?

S. ... or isn't there?

N. Just a minute. (*Clears his throat.*)

B. Are you going to read?

N. As soon as my throat ...

S. You don't want to read?

N. I'll take my shoes off.

B. Read first.

N. When I work I take my shoes off.

S. Let him take them off if he wants to.

N (*takes off his shoes and lays them carefully in a conspicuous place away from the table. He returns and sits down*). Aaahh ... eeee ... It's all smudgy.

B. Hurry up!

N. It's hot! (*Takes off his jacket, hangs it on the back of one of the chairs, returns to the table, puts on the king's mask, sits down.*)

B (*insistently*). Is there going to be a party?

S. ... or isn't there?

N (*reads suspiciously fast, but occasionally his speech falters*). 'And so the edict was pronounced ... and the King declared ... the matter is simple, there is no place for argument ...'

S. What's that? No party?

N (*turning his head away from the book, towards* S). No party? Of course there's a party.

B. There is!

   (S *makes as if to hit* N.)

N. Don't hit me!

S. Read on.

N (*reads*). 'And the King said: "If it please you, the Queen has informed me that concerning the matter of the party ..." '

B. Is there a party?

N. No. No party.

(N *gets up, takes off the king's mask, puts on his shoes. B and
S walk after him in silence. B seizes him by the front of the shirt,
S by the hair.*)

B. Can you read?

N. Can *you*?

(S *and B release him silently and walk away. They take off their
masks and put them on the table. N now unties his tie. S and B
watch him. N takes one of the chairs and puts it against the wall.
He stands on the chair. He ties one end of his tie to a nail in the
wall.*)

B. What's he doing?

S. Aren't you funny?

(N *pulls the loose end of his tie to check that it is firmly fixed.*)

B. Hey, what are you doing?

N (*more to himself than giving a reply*). I've had enough.

S. What do you mean?

N. I can't go on. (*Ties the loose end of his tie into a knot.*)

B. Don't take it to heart.

N. I can't go on without a party.

B (*to S, accusingly*). You see what you've done. The idiot's hanging
himself.

S (*argumentatively*). It's not my fault.

(N *steps off the chair, puts on his jacket.*)

B. What did you say about a party?

S. I'm not giving a party.

(N *carefully adjusts the flower in his buttonhole and steps up on
to the chair again.*)

B (*to N*). Look, stop, will you?

N. What a life!

B. It's not that bad.

N. Without a party?

B. It's possible to live.

N. No, I don't want to.

B (*to S*). This is your fault.

S. It's a bad business.

B (*to N*). Wait!

N. What for?

B. Don't you want to live?

N. I can't live it up, so why live?

B *(to* S). Tell him.

S. Aren't you worried?

N. What am I to do?

S. Aren't you frightened?

N. I couldn't give a damn. (*Puts the noose round his neck.*)

S *(wraps the white dress around him and puts on the mask of death).*
Look at me.

N. Unconvincing.

S *(walks up to N who is standing on the chair, looks up at him).* Have
another look!

N. That's you in between them.

S. What about below the waistline?

N *(less certainly).* I see what you mean. Still, you ...

S. It's not me.

N. It is you.

S. It's not me, it's her.

N. Transvestite.

B. Just hang yourself a little. Not completely. Just a bit.

N. No, I'm going to do it all.

B. Aren't you our friend?

N. We've been around.

B. You're hopeless. (*Puts on the cherry-coloured skirt and the woman's
mask.*) Look!

N. What?

B *(stretching out his arms to N).* Come to me, my angel!

N. A fine time for jokes.

B. Am I not beautiful?

N. You're bald.

B *(to* S). Give me the hair.

S *(puts the wig on B's head).* You look lovely.

N. Transvestites.

B *(in a falsetto voice).* Come, lay your head on my bosom!

N. Nuts!

B (*still in a falsetto voice and embracing him round the legs*). I shall smother you with my embraces.

N (*moves from foot to foot, trying to free himself. He cannot move anything else because of the noose*). Go away! Go and do your Christmas play.

S (*to B, in an advisory tone of voice*). Offer him your burning lips.

N (*in a panic*). No, I don't want to.

S. He'd rather hang himself.

B (*stepping back, in his normal voice*). Come on, what do you want?

N. I want music.

S. Don't we all.

N. I just want them to play one wedding march. Just one wedding march.

B. One of ours?

N. That's right.

B. Loudly?

N. Yes, just for me.

B. Or do you want a waltz?

N. Whichever you like.

B. I'll play you some music.

S. I'll dance.

N. I can't believe it.

B (*throws away the skirt, takes off the mask*). Give me the concertina. (*Runs up to where the concertina is lying on the floor and picks it up.*)

S (*amazed*). What's happening? A party?

B. There's going to be music.

N (*hopefully*). Do you promise?

B. Stop! Enough! We're going to play some music.

N. I'm waiting.

S. By ourselves?

B. What else do we need?

S. We need a party.

B. We'll arrange that. When we start playing, there'll be one.

N. What?

B. A party.

N. Will there really?

B (*to* S). Give him the bottle.
          (S *takes the bottle from under the table, knocks out the cork and*
          gives it to N.)
N. I don't want it yet. Music first!
B. Drink up, my friend, it's a party.
N. I don't want to. I want music.
B. Drink! (N *obediently drinks.*) Faster, faster!
          (N *moves his head backwards, with the bottle at his lips and the*
          noose round his neck. He finishes the bottle and hands it empty
          to S, *who is waiting at the foot of the chair.*)
N (*shouts*). I want music!
B. In a minute. (*To* S.) You dance, right?
S (*hesitating*). You'd better get someone who knows now ...
B (*takes his buttonhole out of his pocket and throws it at* S, *who catches*
          it in the air). Dance, you idiot, dance!
          (S, *still wearing the death mask, stands in the position of a dancer,*
          with one hand on his hip and the other, stretched out, holding the
          buttonhole. He lifts one leg.)
     Three! Four!
          (B *squeezes the concertina, running his fingers up and down the keys.*
          S *slowly begins to dance. But the concertina gives no sound at all.*)
S (*stopping*). Play it!
B (*tries again, but without success*). It's broken.
S. You broke it.
B. You threw it as well as me.
S (*pointing to* N). It wasn't me, it was him.
N. It was both of you.
B. Me? (*Pointing to* S.) You mean him!
N. How long do I have to wait? Mend it! And hurry up!
B. I need a hammer.
          (*In this scene everything happens at a brisk tempo.* S *takes one of*
          N's *shoes off.* N *cannot resist because he is immobilized by the*
          noose. S *gives it to* B.)
S. Use the heel.
N. My new shoes.
B. Good idea! (*Strikes the concertina with the shoe.*)

N. Stop it?

S. We're doing this for you.

> (*Again squeezes the concertina. S gets ready to dance, but the concertina still does not work.*)

B. Not a sound. It must have been broken before we came.

N. Nonsense!

B. Of course it was.

S. Nobody knows.

N. Well, play the double-bass.

B (*opens the case and takes out the double-bass*). Damn it!

N. What?

B. They've taken the strings.

N. Do you promise?

B (*lifts the double-bass in the air with two hands, shouts*). Where are the strings? (*Throws the double-bass on to the floor.*)

N. I want music! I'll hang myself. (*Pause.*) Do you hear me?

S (*taking off the skirt and mask*). Let him hang himself.

N (*amazed*). What's that?

B. Hang himself?

S. Everything's half-cock in this place. First the party, then the funeral.

B. That's not our fault.

S. Everything's nearly, everything's perhaps. Nothing's real.

B. What do you suggest?

S. Let him hang himself.

B. There'll be a funeral.

S. That's the point. I want something real.

B. We came to a party.

S. I know.

B. A funeral isn't a party.

S. Look, we've got to do something. Everything's mixed up. It's so vague.

B. I wanted to play some music but nothing happened.

S. Well, we'll start with a funeral. Maybe a funeral will actually work.

B. We came to a party ...

S. I know. In the end that's what we'll get.

B. A funeral ...

s. It's all the same thing. A funeral's just as good as a wedding. If we help one of them along a bit, things will get better. Otherwise it's all mixed up.

B. Has he got to hang himself?

s. He's got to be *real*.

B (*to* N.) Do you hear?

N. Now listen, boys ...

B. You're in trouble, my friend.

s. Just carry on. We'll wait.

N (*disbelievingly*). You want me to hang myself?

B. You heard what he said?

N. Hang myself? Seriously?

B. You suggested it.

N (*frees himself from the noose, steps off the chair*). I've changed my mind.

B. You're forgetting what you said.

s. You don't want to?

N. Certainly not.

B. Are you trying to spoil our party?
   (N *detaches his tie from the nail.*)

s. You promised.

N. Not really. (*Ties his tie round his neck again.*)

B. He's spoiling everything!

s. I told you, didn't I? It's all half-and-half; nothing's real.

B. Aren't you ashamed of yourself?

N. Leave me alone.

B (*to* S.) Don't you think we ought to ...

s. We've *got* to. (*They walk up to* N.)

N. What do you want?

B. It's for your own good ... (*They take him by the arms.*)

N. Go away!

s. We don't hold it against you.

B. We're your friends.

s. We must stick together.

B. So *you* hang yourself ...

N. I don't want to!

B. What?

N. Let me go!

B. He doesn't respect reality.

S. We'll help him. (*They carry him towards the wall.*)

N. I'll play music on my comb ...

B. You drank all that vodka. You haven't done so badly. (*They take his tie off.*)

N (*resisting*). It was a wedding feast.

B (*putting the king's mask on* N). We'll hang him like a king.

N. Wait! The party's going to start now.

B. What? When it's not real?

S. We must have our reality.

N. I don't want to.

S. Don't lose your temper. (*They reach the wall.*)

B. We only want what's real. Nothing's possible without reality.
   (*A pause while* S *and* B *try to carry out their wishes.* N *resists, but the others have complete superiority over him. They act entirely without malice, pleasantly and with an air of ownership. Then from far away they hear a typical village band: a drum, a trumpet or flute, a violin and a double-bass. They are playing a slow, sentimental waltz.*)

N. Music!
   (*Pause. They listen intently.*)

B (*joyfully*). Music!
   (S *and* B *move away from* N. N *takes the king's mask off his head.*)

S. Where is it?

B. It's not here.

S. Where is it, if it's not here?

B. Somewhere else.

S. There isn't anywhere else.

N. The party's over there.

S. Who's it for?

S AND N (*together*). Where's the party?

B (*in the middle of the stage, facing the audience, hands in the air*). Ladies! Gentlemen! Where is the party?

Enchanted
Night

Translated from the Polish *Czarowna Noc*

Characters

Old Boy

Old Man

Third Person

When the curtain rises the stage is dark except for a faint red light far away in the distance. There are sounds of a key turning in a lock and the click of a switch. A harsh, bright light, hanging from the ceiling, is turned on. OLD BOY and OLD MAN are standing in the doorway.

The setting is a room in a medium-class hotel. In the right-hand wall (from the audience's point of view) is the door through which OLD BOY and OLD MAN have just entered. Farther upstage stands a coat-rack.

The back wall – from right to left – has a side door leading into the next room, blocked by a chest of drawers with a mirror on top. Beside the mirror is a framed, glazed photograph of the Venus de Milo, with a broad white margin. Next to that is the first iron bedstead, its head against the wall and its foot towards the audience. A short distance away is the second bed, identical and arranged in the same way. Between the beds is a standard lamp. Above the beds is a large oil-painting of a bouquet of roses.

In the left wall: some way upstage, is a tall narrow window with a lace curtain and shutters, which are now pushed to one side. It is through this window that the red light is shining. It is a signal from a near-by railway line. A little nearer the front of the stage is a screen with a wash-basin behind it. The screen should not block the audience's view of the window, although it is placed beside the same wall as the window and near the front of the stage. In the middle of the room is a table, on which are a telephone, a two-branched candlestick with two candles in it, and a box of matches.

OLD BOY and OLD MAN are men in the prime of life. They are typical middle-rank officials or white-collar workers, well qualified, travelling for some conference or delegation. OLD MAN is not, in fact, OLD BOY's immediate superior, but he seems to be a man of higher standing or to have greater responsibility. On the other hand intimacy has been forced upon them by their having to travel together. Their dress and equipment

*are typical of members of a delegation: they have coats and hats, and
not much luggage – bags rather than suitcases.*

OLD BOY. Which bed, old man?

OLD MAN. You choose, old boy.

OLD BOY. Oh no, please, you have first pick.

OLD MAN. No no. After you. Which one?

OLD BOY. I don't mind.

OLD MAN. It's all the same to me.

OLD BOY. Me too.

OLD MAN. I couldn't care less.

OLD BOY. Nor could I.

    (*They stand for a moment stalemated. They are very tired.*)

OLD MAN (*with a note of impatience*). Which one, then?

OLD BOY. No, really … I promise you, I …

OLD MAN. All right, old boy. If you don't mind I'll take this one
    here, O.K.?

OLD BOY. Fine, go ahead.

OLD MAN. That's very kind of you, old boy.

OLD BOY (*throws his bag on to the second bed, the one nearer the window*).
    My feet are killing me.

OLD MAN. Sleep … Beautiful sleep.

OLD BOY (*sits down on the bed and takes off his shoes*). What a relief!

    (OLD MAN *sits down carefully on the first bed which emits the
    long drawn-out moan of a broken spring.*)

OLD MAN. Old boy, er, if it's all the same to you …

OLD BOY (*cheerfully*). Anything you like, old man.

OLD MAN. Then perhaps you wouldn't mind changing places
    with me, old boy.

OLD BOY. Change places?

OLD MAN. Yes. I'd rather be by the window. Fresh air, you
    know …

OLD BOY (*worriedly*). What is it? Are the legs a bit … ?

OLD MAN. Oh no, nothing like that. It's just that at home I always
    sleep next to the window. I like it by the window. (*Another
    spring noise.*)

OLD BOY. Shall we change?

OLD MAN. If you don't mind ...

OLD BOY. Of course, with pleasure!

(*They both stand up.* OLD BOY *grabs hold of the railing of his bed and drags it into the middle of the room.*)

OLD MAN. What are you doing?

OLD BOY. You wanted to change places, so I'm changing ...

OLD MAN. Yes, I know, but it's such a business. Please don't trouble, old boy.

OLD BOY. No trouble at all, old man. (*Pushes the broken bed into the empty space by the window.*) Everyone has their little preferences, I can understand. It's quite natural that you want to be by the window. There we are. All ready and waiting.

OLD MAN (*acidly*). You're terribly kind.

OLD BOY (*takes off his coat and hat, hangs them up; unbuttons his collar and takes off his tie in front of the mirror; catches sight of the* Venus de Milo, *gives a slight whistle.* OLD MAN *jumps nervously*). What's the matter?

OLD MAN. You whistled.

OLD BOY. Yes, I know. What about it?

OLD MAN. I'm allergic.

OLD BOY. Oh.

OLD MAN. I can't stand people whistling. Whistle-phobia. Ever since I was a child. I was born with it.

OLD BOY. Forgive me. I'm terribly sorry. I didn't know.

OLD MAN. A very rare case. Over-sensitive ear-drums.

OLD BOY. I really must apologize.

OLD MAN. Don't worry. It doesn't matter.

OLD BOY. I whistled because I noticed something. Have you seen this? (*Points to the* Venus de Milo.)

OLD MAN (*walks up to the photograph.*) Ah, the ancient world!

OLD BOY. Not bad, is she?

OLD MAN. For me it is a work of art.

OLD BOY. You don't think she's got something?

OLD MAN. I'm a married man.

OLD BOY. So am I, old man, so am I. Who do you think I live

with, my old grandma? But here we are, away from home for this conference, and we can have a little joke – man to man.

OLD MAN. My dear boy, it's a picture.

OLD BOY. Yes, but there's something about it.

OLD MAN. It's a photograph, and not even a natural photograph. A photograph of a sculpture and probably of a plaster cast of it. A picture of a copy. And this copy is in all likelihood copied from yet another copy. It is only then that we come to the original. And the original is marble, old boy, nothing more. And before the marble ...

OLD BOY. Yes? Go on.

OLD MAN. An idea in the mind of the artist.

OLD BOY. And before that?

OLD MAN. Before what?

OLD BOY. Before the artist's idea?

OLD MAN. Well, in the final resort, I suppose ...

OLD BOY. You see, old man. Exactly. I told you there was something in it.

OLD MAN. Imagination, old boy. Imagination ...

OLD BOY. Oh, forget it. (*Takes off his tie and jacket, throws them on one of the chairs.*) Are you washing?

OLD MAN. Yes, but you first, old man, if you don't mind. I'll wait.

OLD BOY. I won't be a moment. (*Takes his bag and disappears behind the screen. After a moment sounds of flowing water and of splashing and snorting can be heard. A towel appears and is hung over the screen.* OLD MAN *stands in front of the* Venus de Milo, *still wearing his hat.*)
    I wonder who left this soap here.

OLD MAN (*abstractedly*). What soap?

OLD BOY. On the wash-basin.

OLD MAN. I suppose the man who stayed here before us.

OLD BOY. Don't they tidy up after people? (*More splashing.*) It's scented ...

OLD MAN. What?

OLD BOY. The soap. (OLD BOY's *bare arms appear from behind the screen holding a piece of soap.*) Try it.

OLD MAN (*sniffs*). You're right.

OLD BOY. Violets.

OLD MAN. Not violets. Lilac.

OLD BOY. I'd say it was violets.

OLD MAN. Have a proper sniff.

(*The hand with the soap returns behind the screen. There are sounds of loud sniffing.*)

OLD BOY. Mmmmm-haaaa ... Yes, definitely ... I still think it's violets.

OLD MAN. The smell of lilac is more distinctive.

OLD BOY. I like violets.

OLD MAN. Put it down. It's unhygienic.

OLD BOY (*gargles noisily*). Don't you like violets, old man?

OLD MAN. No. I prefer lilac.

OLD BOY (*comes out from behind the screen in striped pyjamas and stockinged feet, carrying his clothes on his arm*). You getting undressed, old man? (*Throws his clothes carelessly on the chair.*)

OLD MAN. Ah, yes of course. (*Takes off his coat and hat, hangs them up. Takes off his jacket and hangs it on the other chair. Walks up to the mirror again to untie his tie.*) Have you noticed, old boy, this mirror distorts your reflection?

OLD BOY. Impossible!

OLD MAN. It's frightfully distorting.

OLD BOY. Optical illusion, perhaps?

OLD MAN. Illusion? What do you mean? You check it yourself. Look at me.

OLD BOY. All right.

OLD MAN. Have you looked?

OLD BOY. Yes.

OLD MAN. Now look at my reflection in the mirror. Oh, oh.

OLD BOY. Mmmm, yes, definitely.

OLD MAN. Distorts, doesn't it?

OLD BOY. No.

OLD MAN. What do you mean, no?

OLD BOY. That is to say ... yes. A little bit.

OLD MAN. A little bit! You're standing wrong. You can't see

properly. Come here and stand where I am. (*Takes* OLD BOY *by the arm and leads him to where he was standing.*) Now take a good look. Can you see yourself?

OLD BOY. Yes. It's incredible.

OLD MAN. Does it distort?

OLD BOY. Disgracefully. What a rotten mirror.

OLD MAN. You see.

(*They both walk away sadly into the middle of the room.*)

OLD BOY. It's intolerable.

OLD MAN. They weren't like that in the old days. (*Takes his bag and vanishes behind the screen. A second towel appears beside the first.*)

OLD BOY (*sits on his bed, thinking*). How could he have imagined ...

OLD MAN (*shouting above the noise of the water*). What did you say, old boy?

OLD BOY. Er, no ... nothing.

(*Bubbles rise from behind the screen.*)

OLD MAN. I thought you spoke. (*From below there comes the dull, soft sound of a band playing a foxtrot.*) What's that music?

OLD BOY. There's a restaurant and a dance club on the floor below. (OLD MAN *resumes his noises behind the screen.*) Do you like music, old man?

(*There is no answer.* OLD MAN *apparently does not hear the question.* OLD BOY, *having first convinced himself that* OLD MAN *is well occupied in his washing, picks up his pillow and feels it. He finds that it is thin and feeble. He secretly checks the pillow on* OLD MAN'S *bed, compares them and then quickly changes the pillows over. He then quickly jumps on to his own bed and closes his eyes.* OLD MAN *comes out from behind the screen in striped pyjamas, carrying his bag and his clothes.*)

OLD MAN (*briskly*). Well, time for beddybyes! (OLD BOY *is pretending to be asleep.*) I hope there are no bugs around. I'm a light sleeper. What's that? (*Lays his clothes down into an immaculate pile.*) You know, old boy, we've got to get up early again tomorrow. Still, we can sleep it off at home. What day is it now? How do you manage to get any sleep with these bugs crawling around? What did you say, old boy? The poor man's exhausted. (*Makes as if to fling himself on to his bed, but remembers that it is broken. Lies down on it carefully. Gives a deep sigh of relief when, in spite of his fears, the bed supports his weight and nothing terrible happens.*) This is luxury. (*Pause.*) We'd better have the light off. (*Only now does he realize that* OLD BOY *is not answering him and not moving. He repeats more loudly.*) We'd better have the light off! (OLD BOY *emits an ostentatious snore.* OLD MAN *leans across from his bed and pulls him by the arm.*) Old boy!

OLD BOY (*stretching and yawning*). Oh, it's you ...

OLD MAN (*with a friendly, knowing smile*). Bed at last, eh? (OLD BOY *turns over on to his side.* OLD MAN *shakes his arm again.* OLD BOY *raises his head.*) At last we can get some sleep, eh?

OLD BOY (*intending to collapse once again*). Aha ...

OLD MAN (*hurriedly*). Only someone's got to turn the light off.

OLD BOY. I turned it off last time.

OLD MAN. Did you?

OLD BOY. Yesterday, in that last hotel.

OLD MAN. Aaah, of course, of course ...

OLD BOY. Exactly.

OLD MAN. Old boy, don't be pedantic. You're nearer the switch.

OLD BOY. I'm not really. It's an illusion of perspective.

OLD MAN. Don't let's quibble, old boy. I'd get up myself, but you're obviously nearer.

OLD BOY. I haven't got any socks on.

OLD MAN. Come on! You were in the army. On your feet, one two, one two, and you're there.

OLD BOY (*unenthusiastically*). One two, one two ... (*Gets up and walks to the door where the switch is. In the distance the orchestra begins to play a sentimental tango.* OLD BOY *turns round to face the room so as to remember the way back to his bed and raises his hand towards the switch. He notices the side door.*) There's another door there.

OLD MAN. Where?

OLD BOY. Behind the chest of drawers.

OLD MAN. This must have been a two-room suite once.

(OLD BOY *goes to the door behind the chest of drawers and gently tries to turn the door-knob.*)

OLD BOY. It's locked.

OLD MAN. Well, that's quite right.

(OLD BOY *moves the chest of drawers aside a little and peeps through the key-hole.*)

OLD BOY. I can't see anything. It's blocked up with paper.

OLD MAN. Of course. They always block them up. (OLD BOY *walks over to his clothes which are laid out on the chair and takes a pencil out of his jacket.*) What are you doing, old boy?

OLD BOY. I'm going to see what we can do about it. (*Goes back to the concealed door and pushes the pencil through the keyhole, then looks through.*)

OLD MAN. Old boy, don't be stupid! (OLD BOY *peeps through the key-hole.*) Put the light out and go to sleep. You're supposed to be a responsible citizen. (*Pause.*) Old boy, I can understand that when you're still at school, you ... But now? You're the head of a family . (OLD BOY *begins to giggle.*) What is it?

OLD BOY (*giggles and slaps his thighs*). Well I never!

OLD MAN. What can you see? (OLD BOY *does not answer, just giggles. OLD MAN gets up and joins him at the key-hole.*) What is it?

OLD BOY. Ho-ho! What have we here?!

OLD MAN. Show me! (OLD BOY *pays no attention to him.*) Move out of the way!

OLD BOY. Well I'll be d ...

OLD MAN. Hey! Let's have a look. (OLD BOY, *wearing an idiot smile, gives up his place. OLD MAN bends down to the key-hole, then straightens himself up with dignity.*) You ought to be ashamed of yourself!

(OLD BOY *tries to occupy the point of observation, but OLD MAN bends down quickly and gets there first.*)

OLD BOY. It's my turn.

OLD MAN. Just a minute.

OLD BOY. I was here first.

(*They elbow each other aside. At last OLD BOY manages to get to the key-hole. The orchestra finishes playing the tango.*)

OLD MAN. Come on, tell me. (OLD BOY *does not answer.*) What is it? Don't keep me in suspense. (OLD BOY *stops looking and walks away silently.*) What happened? (OLD BOY *does not answer.*) Tell me, what happened?

OLD BOY. He turned round.

OLD MAN. What?

OLD BOY. It was a man.

OLD MAN. Impossible! How do you know?

OLD BOY. What do you mean? Do you think I'm an idiot?

OLD MAN. Hmm ... (*Without a word* OLD BOY *lies down on his bed. Both men avoid each other's glance.*) Hmm. Yes. (*Pause.*) An exceptionally warm night, don't you think? What was I going to say? Ah, yes, old boy, I think tonight we shall leave the window open ... yeees. Good night.

OLD BOY (*gloomily*). Good night.

> (OLD MAN *turns the light off. The stage is completely dark except for one single red point of light, outside the window.* OLD MAN *also climbs into bed. A slightly longer pause, during which both men are asleep; they should not emit exaggerated snores at this time. The stage gradually gets a little lighter, in the same way that the human eye grows accustomed to darkness. The lighting of the stage must correspond exactly with this optical effect. From out of the silence the sound of a moving train can be heard, and suddenly there is the piercing whistle of a steam engine, its loudness out of all proportion to the noise of the train's wheels. It seems to come from right under the window.* OLD MAN *jerks himself awake and sits up in bed.*)

OLD MAN. What's that? What was that? (*There is another whistle, but farther away. After a moment the sound of the wheels also grows quieter, then vanishes completely.* OLD BOY *is still sleeping soundly.* OLD MAN *leans out of bed towards him.*) Old boy? (*Silence.*) ... I say, old boy ... (*Silence.* OLD MAN *waits for a moment and then grabs his colleague by the arm.*)

OLD BOY (*waking up violently*). Yes! Today! Today! Absolutely! I insist!

OLD MAN (*calming him*). It's me, old boy, it's me.

OLD BOY (*regaining consciousness*). Oh, it's you.

OLD MAN. Were you dreaming?

OLD BOY. No, nothing important ...

OLD MAN. I'm terribly sorry to wake you up, old boy, but there's a railway line outside the window.

OLD BOY. What about it?

OLD MAN. I didn't know about it. Er, old boy, would you mind doing me a favour and changing places? That is, if it doesn't make any difference to you. You see, I'm allergic to whistles. It's my heart ... If it's not too much trouble I'd rather be farther away from the window.

OLD BOY. Why not shut the window?

OLD MAN. We'd suffocate. It's a stifling hot night.

OLD BOY. You're right. It's hot as hell.

OLD MAN. I'm really most frightfully sorry, old boy.

OLD BOY (*with forced politeness*). It doesn't matter. Don't worry about it at all.

OLD MAN. Do forgive me, please.

OLD BOY. There's nothing to forgive.

OLD MAN. I must apologize.

OLD BOY. Please! It's not important.

OLD MAN (*down to business*). And you don't mind changing places?

OLD BOY (*with conventional politeness, bordering on fury*). With the greatest of pleasure. I'd be delighted ... delighted. (*Turns on the standard lamp and gets ready to drag the beds into their new positions.*)

OLD MAN (*transfers himself swiftly to the other bed*). No, please, don't bother to move it. We'll just change the sheets. That's all we need do.

OLD BOY. Fine! Anything you say! (*Works off his anger by changing the sheets. After that the men stretch themselves out on their beds. The bed under the window creaks horribly, this time under the weight of* OLD BOY, *and he lets out a cry of pain.*)

OLD MAN. Are you quite comfortable?

OLD BOY. Oh yes, thank you.

OLD MAN. What was that noise?

OLD BOY. A spring.

OLD MAN. I'm frightfully grateful to you, old boy, I really am.

OLD BOY. The pleasure is entirely mine.

OLD MAN. Let's get some sleep, then. Good night.

OLD BOY. Good night.

(OLD MAN *turns off the light. As before the stage is completely dark and then gradually grows lighter. Both men are asleep. A train is heard approaching, then a whistle, the same as before. Both men jerk themselves up in bed simultaneously.*)

OLD MAN. You awake too?

OLD BOY. Are you surprised?

OLD MAN. You're not allergic.

OLD BOY. But I'm next to the window. (*Noise of the departing train and another whistle, now some way off.*)

OLD MAN. My God!

OLD BOY. Oh Lord!

OLD MAN. That railway line must be just outside. What do you think?

OLD BOY. They're completely thoughtless the way they build these things.

OLD MAN. What shall we do?

OLD BOY. I've no idea. We'd better shut the window.

OLD MAN. It'll be stifling.

OLD BOY. Would you rather wake up every five minutes?

OLD MAN. Well, you'd better shut it then.

OLD BOY. Me?

OLD MAN. I turned the light off.

OLD BOY. Yes, of course.

OLD MAN. You'll be better at shutting it. You're the engineer and I'm the economist.

OLD BOY. Yes, I suppose so.

OLD MAN. And besides, you're nearer the window. (OLD BOY *gets up and walks over to the window. Suddenly he leaps back.*) Have you closed it?

OLD BOY. Shhh ...

OLD MAN. What? Won't it shut? (OLD BOY *puts his hand over the*

other man's mouth. OLD MAN *mumbles through the fingers.*) What
are you doing?

OLD BOY (*whispers*). Keep quiet, for Christ's sake. There's some-
body there! (*Loosens his grip.*)

OLD MAN (*whispers*). Where?

OLD BOY (*whispers*). There, in the corner.

OLD MAN (*whispers*). You must be imagining it.

OLD BOY (*whispers*). Go and look for yourself. (*Pause.*)

OLD MAN (*whispers*). Give me the telephone.

OLD BOY (*whispers*). What for?

OLD MAN (*whispers*). I'm going to ring reception. You bring it
here and I'll ring.

OLD BOY (*whispers*). No?

OLD MAN (*whispers*). You're already up.

OLD BOY (*whispers*). I had to shut the window. It's your turn.
(*Pause.*)

OLD MAN (*whispers.*) Shall I turn the light on?

OLD BOY (*aloud*). No! For God's sake! (*Whispers.*) If he's got a
gun he'll see us as clear as day. (*The shadow of a third person
appears.*) He's moving. (OLD BOY *jumps on to* OLD MAN'*s bed,
it being the one nearer to him.*)

VOICE OF THE THIRD PERSON (*a young, female voice*). Is it you?

OLD BOY (*whispers*). Who's she talking to?

OLD MAN (*whispers*). I thought she was your friend!

THIRD PERSON. Why don't you answer?

OLD MAN (*whispers*). For Christ's sake say something.

OLD BOY (*whispers*). What shall I say?

OLD MAN (*whispers*). Anything you like.

OLD BOY (*emits a sound such as well-brought-up people use to call
to each other in woods*). Cu-ckoo!

THIRD PERSON. Don't be silly. Where are you?

OLD BOY. Here! Under the blankets!

OLD MAN (*whispers*). Idiot!

OLD BOY (*whispers*). You talk to her yourself, then.

THIRD PERSON. Wait, I'll turn the light on.

OLD MAN (*in a panic*). No!

OLD BOY. No, no, please, don't turn it on.

THIRD PERSON. I must see you.

OLD BOY. I haven't shaved.

OLD MAN. No! Neither have I.

THIRD PERSON (*laughing*). Don't worry about that. You're like a child!

(THIRD PERSON *strikes a match and lights the two candles. The orchestra begins to play a slow rhythmical melody. The* THIRD PERSON *is a young girl in a strapless dress, deeply décolleté, close-fitting at the waist, widening from the hips into a foamy crinoline made of tulle and sequins. She is the answer to a middle-aged man's dream. But the production must make sure that she is not a vulgar person either in appearance or in behaviour. She is wearing 'pin-heels' but her footsteps cannot be heard either now or later. Her hair is dressed in a chignon, leaving the back of her neck uncovered.* THIRD PERSON *takes the candelabra in one hand and walks towards the bed.* OLD MAN *and* OLD BOY *are on the bed together. She raises the candelabra and illuminates them. They are sitting side by side, half under the blankets, dishevelled and blinking their eyes. They cannot help looking idiotic.*)

OLD BOY (*resignedly*). Good evening, madam.

OLD MAN. Precisely.

OLD BOY. May I introduce myself.

OLD MAN (*smoothing his hair back nervously*). If you will permit me, madam, ...

OLD BOY (*nudges* OLD MAN). Introduce me, old man.

OLD MAN. Madam, may I present my colleague ...

(OLD BOY *bows, but because he is sitting up in bed this looks a little awkward.*)

OLD BOY. How do you do, madam.

OLD MAN (*quietly*). Now you do me.

OLD BOY. ... and this is my friend ... (OLD MAN *bows.*)

OLD MAN. How do you do.

THIRD PERSON. Why are there two of you?

OLD MAN. We're always together ... it's a delegation ...

OLD BOY. But we're quite separate really.

THIRD PERSON (*wagging her finger at them in jest*). You've been playing a trick on me!

OLD BOY (*gallantly, pointing to the chair*). Would you like to sit down?

OLD MAN. Do sit down, please.

THIRD PERSON (*returning to the centre of the room*). Why didn't you tell me?

> (*The men realize that the chairs are occupied by their clothes. Together they jump out of bed and feverishly grab their things off the chairs. They do not know where to put them and hide them behind their backs.*)

OLD MAN. Would you like a cup of tea?

OLD BOY (*quietly*). You know there isn't any tea.

OLD MAN. No, don't have tea if you don't want any.

> (*Meanwhile* THIRD PERSON *sits on the table.*)

OLD BOY (*backing away towards his bed and quickly packing his things away under the blankets*). I'm afraid it's a bit of a mess here.

OLD MAN (*doing the same*). Bachelor life, ha, ha ...

THIRD PERSON. But at last I have found you. Isn't it wonderful!

OLD MAN (*uncertainly pointing to himself*). Me?

THIRD PERSON. I searched for you everywhere. And I've found you.

OLD MAN. I'm so sorry, I ... I've been travelling, you see. Trips and journeys all the time. On business, you know. (*Pause.*)

THIRD PERSON (*slightly at a loss, in the tone of a friendly, conventional conversation*). And now it's summer again ...

OLD MAN. I know. You can feel it even at night-time. (OLD BOY *makes signs to him.*) Yesterday I sweated so much I thought I was going to die. (*To* OLD BOY.) What is it?

OLD BOY (*quietly*). Come here.

OLD MAN (*unwillingly*). Just a minute. Excuse me, madam, I must have a word with my colleague. (*Walks towards* OLD BOY.)

THIRD PERSON (*sighing, to herself*). Summer, summer, summer ...
> (*Lifts her arms, takes the comb out of her hair and lets it down.*)

OLD MAN. What do you want?

OLD BOY. Who is this person?

OLD MAN. I've no idea.

OLD BOY. Honestly?

OLD MAN. Yes, honestly, I've never seen her before in my life.

OLD BOY. So how do you know she's talking to *you*?

OLD MAN. Well she is, isn't she?

OLD BOY. You said a moment ago you didn't know her.

OLD MAN. I don't know her.

OLD BOY. Well then?

OLD MAN. You don't know her either.

OLD BOY. You're trying to pick her up!

OLD MAN. I'm not trying to pick her up. I'm just maintaining the conversation. I was well brought up.

(*The orchestra begins playing an old-fashioned waltz.*)

OLD BOY. Now listen, old man, I ...

OLD MAN. Wait!

OLD BOY. What's the matter?

OLD MAN. Can't you smell anything?

OLD BOY. Where?

OLD MAN. Here, in the room. It's lilac.

OLD BOY. Aha!

OLD MAN. A smell of lilac.

OLD BOY. Only it's not lilac, it's violets.

OLD MAN. Lilac! It's quite distinct.

THIRD PERSON (*who has meanwhile been standing in front of the mirror, looking at herself and doing her hair with long strokes of her comb*). What are you doing? (OLD MAN *and* OLD BOY *look at each other in alarm.*) Come here. Come to me. (*Both men walk uncertainly towards her.*) You look beautiful in those pyjamas. Let me see you.

OLD MAN. Me?

OLD BOY. Me?

THIRD PERSON. Turn round! (*Both men turn completely round.*) Mmmm! You're so good-looking.

OLD BOY. Oh ... er ... I'm not really.

OLD MAN. Er ... maybe my profile.

THIRD PERSON. Most of all I adore your eyes. There's something so scintillating and attractive ...

OLD BOY. We-eel, sometimes, perhaps.

OLD MAN (*solemnly*). It's a matter of character.

THIRD PERSON. When I look at you, I melt into your body. I am no longer myself. My eyes become yours, my mouth changes into your mouth. I can't control my desires. Come to me, my darling – don't you want to? Mmmm, come! (*Stretches out her arms and embraces both men around the neck.*)

OLD BOY. Push off, will you, old man.

OLD MAN. You push off. Can't you see I'm with a woman?

OLD BOY. Honestly, old man, you're married. Don't you remember?

OLD MAN. That's right. (*Tries to free himself from her embrace.*) Excuse me, please, let me go.

THIRD PERSON. I long for you. Can you understand that?

OLD MAN (*stops trying to free himself*). You see, old boy? What am I to do?

OLD BOY. She's not talking to you.

OLD MAN. Well who is she talking to?

OLD BOY. Don't start all that again.

OLD MAN. I'm not starting anything.

OLD BOY. Exactly! Don't forget, you're not the only person here.

OLD MAN. Nor are you.

THIRD PERSON. You're boring me. (*Stops embracing them, walks to one side, takes off her shoes.*)

OLD BOY. What's going on?

OLD MAN. She must think we're someone else.

OLD BOY. At this distance? Out of the question. You don't know life, old man.

OLD MAN. So what is your opinion?

OLD BOY. I am beginning to think ...

OLD MAN. Well, what is it?

OLD BOY. Just a minute ... I know how to find out the truth. Do you want me to?

OLD MAN (*enthusiastically*). Yes, of course. (*Less enthusiastically*). But don't forget, I was against the idea.

(OLD BOY *approaches the* THIRD PERSON, *takes her hand, lifts*

it up in the air and takes a step back. THIRD PERSON *is a little sur-*
prised, but she smiles and does not lower her hand. OLD BOY
puts her other hand in the same position. THIRD PERSON *does not*
move. She is posed unnaturally, like a statue.)

OLD BOY. Yes, I see.

OLD MAN. Is she asleep?

OLD BOY. No, she's not asleep.

OLD MAN. What is it, then?

OLD BOY. She doesn't exist.

OLD MAN. Listen, old boy, this is no time for jokes. I am your
senior in the office, you know.

OLD BOY. It's not a joke. She doesn't exist because she's a dream.
What's so strange about that? It's one o'clock.

OLD MAN. Nonsense!

OLD BOY. Don't you ever dream, old man?

OLD MAN. Yes I do, but ... but not like that.

OLD BOY. What *do* you mean, old man? Don't you think I know
what I'm talking about?

OLD MAN. Can I trust you?

OLD BOY. Implicitly. Anyway I'm completely in your hands. I'm
dreaming as well as you.

OLD MAN. Oh, I see! (*Begins to laugh. Claps* OLD BOY *on the shoulder,*
sits down on the chair.) A stroke of luck for us, eh? She's laughing!
(THIRD PERSON *lowers her arms and begins to laugh as well.*)

OLD BOY. So what? Let her laugh. Don't you realize that in a
dream everything is possible?

THIRD PERSON. Aren't you a funny one!

OLD MAN. Did you hear?

OLD BOY. It doesn't mean anything. In a dream nothing means
anything.

OLD MAN. It's all very well to say that. Maybe it doesn't mean
anything to you, but I'm an important official, with a public
duty to perform.

OLD BOY (*irritated*). What are your dreams usually like, then?

OLD MAN. That's my business.

(*Pause.* OLD BOY *looks at him suspiciously.*)

OLD BOY. Aha, I'm beginning to understand.

OLD MAN (*worried*). What are you beginning to understand?

(THIRD PERSON *walks about the room, gazing at the walls, pictures and furniture.*)

OLD BOY. Nothing, nothing.

OLD MAN (*even more worried*). Please, old boy, tell me.

OLD BOY (*to himself*). Shall I tell him? Well, why not?

OLD MAN. Exactly. Well done. What is it, then?

OLD BOY. It's quite obvious. You're part of my dream.

OLD MAN. Me? On the contrary. You're part of my dream.

OLD BOY. Of course! Funny I didn't think of it sooner. You're in my dream as well as her. I'm dreaming, this room, this night, everything. It's all a dream, it's a dream! (*Feverishly paces from one end of the room to the other.*)

OLD MAN. Nonsense! This is a double room, and I have just the same right to dream as you have.

OLD BOY (*paying no attention to him*). I ought to have thought of it from the start. I had my suspicions of you.

OLD MAN. No, really, I protest. You must not forget, I occupy a responsible position. You are not dreaming about me.

OLD BOY. I am dreaming about you.

OLD MAN. I am not dreaming ... no, what I mean is, I am dreaming, but it's not you about me, it's me about you.

OLD BOY. Why are you getting so upset? Why did you say none of this mattered to you? And why am I not getting upset? If you were dreaming and not me, it wouldn't matter a bit to you whether she's laughing at you or at me or at anyone. The one who's dreaming doesn't ask questions. What do you say to that?

OLD MAN. You're not getting upset, old boy?

OLD BOY. Not in the slightest.

OLD MAN. I don't believe you.

OLD BOY. Shall I prove it?

OLD MAN. Certainly.

(THIRD PERSON *amuses herself pulling out the items of clothing that are hidden under the blankets.*)

OLD BOY. Right ... Now that I know I'm dreaming about you, I'll tell you just what I think of you. You think I don't know why you wanted to change beds, eh? You wanted to make me into a cripple. As soon as that spring went I knew what your little game was, you swindler. And all that waking up in the night. Anyone would think I was your paid servant. 'Turn the light off,' 'Shut the window,' 'Do this,' 'Do that.' And while we're on the subject I'll tell you what I think of your career; but before that I'll describe what your face looks like, and so as to remove all shadow of doubt ...

OLD MAN. Wa-wa-wa-wa ...

OLD BOY (*suddenly thrown out of his stride*). What's that?

OLD MAN. Old boy. Let me ask you just one question. Are you absolutely certain you're dreaming about me?

OLD BOY. I'm ... Why do you ask?

OLD MAN. Well, if you are, fair enough. Don't let it bother you for a minute. All I want to ask you is, are you certain? (*Pause.*)

OLD BOY. Why do you ask?

OLD MAN. If I was dreaming correctly, you said something very strange just then. In front of a lady too.

OLD BOY. I didn't say a word!

OLD MAN. Oh, well, in that case it's all right.

THIRD PERSON (*opening a wallet which has fallen from one of the jackets*). Angel, this photo isn't like you at all.

OLD BOY. Look!

THIRD PERSON. You've got such pretty, round little ears ...

OLD MAN. Whose is that wallet?

OLD BOY. Either mine, or yours.

OLD MAN. Hmmm ... well, it doesn't matter whose it is. (*Both men begin to stride about the stage.*) I just want to point out that if it really is your dream, then you must bear the responsibility for it ...

THIRD PERSON (*laughing*). Ooo-hooo. What a scream!

  (OLD MAN *suddenly flings himself upon her in order to get back his wallet.* THIRD PERSON *opens her arms and* OLD MAN *falls headlong into them. They roll around on the bed – the one nearer*

the door. THIRD PERSON *embraces* OLD MAN *laughing all the time.*
OLD MAN *tears himself away, although he still wants to get
his wallet back. The band begins playing a violent rock-'n'-roll
tune.*)

OLD MAN. Give it to me, please.

THIRD PERSON. Darling!

OLD MAN. I'll call the police.

THIRD PERSON. My angel!

OLD MAN. I'll have you arrested. I refuse to be blackmailed.

THIRD PERSON. You adorable thing!

OLD MAN. I've got a wife! I've got children!

THIRD PERSON. Shhh, quiet, my little rosebud!

    (OLD MAN *manages to get the wallet out of* THIRD PERSON'S
hand. OLD BOY *runs round them like a referee round a pair of
boxers.*)

OLD MAN. Help me, can't you, old boy. I can't get rid of this hell-
cat.

    (OLD BOY *gives him his hand.*)

OLD BOY. Up you come! (*Pulls* OLD MAN *off the bed.*)

OLD MAN. Whew! Family before everything, I say. Please accept
my thanks, old boy.

OLD BOY. Don't mention it. I did it for your children. (OLD
MAN *opens the wallet, throws it on the floor and runs back to* THIRD
PERSON.) What are you doing?

OLD MAN. It's not my wallet at all. It's yours! (*Embraces* THIRD
PERSON.)

OLD BOY. Oh! I see! (*Grabs* OLD MAN *by the leg and tries to pull
him off the bed.*)

OLD MAN. Let go, will you. There's no need to now.

OLD BOY. You think you can do what you like, do you?

OLD MAN. Let go! Don't you see, you're not here?! It's a dream,
it's all a dream!

OLD BOY. Nuts!

OLD MAN. It's me who's dreaming. Me! Me! Where are you,
my lovely one? What is your name? It's me, your little sparrow!

    (THIRD PERSON *gets away from* OLD MAN *and sits on the chair*

*by the table, her legs crossed. She begins to ponder, and later in
her pondering she takes the matches from the table and amuses
herself putting their ends in the candle flame. The orchestra stops
playing rock-'n'-roll. Applause and far-off shouts of 'bravo, bravo'.
It is the end of the dance.*)

OLD BOY. 'Sparrow'! You ought to be ashamed of yourself! At
your age, and with your stomach!

OLD MAN. What are you doing here?

OLD BOY. Still asking silly questions?

OLD MAN. Who are you, anyway?

OLD BOY. What do you mean?

OLD MAN. When I'm dreaming I don't have friends. Come back
in the daytime.

OLD BOY. Listen, old man ...

OLD MAN. Why are you still here? Will you please get out of my
dream at once!

OLD BOY. Now then, old man, let's be sensible.

OLD MAN. Stop chattering and go away!

OLD BOY (*becoming angry*). What's that? You think *you're* dreaming?

OLD MAN. Certainly!

OLD BOY. Well you're not!

OLD MAN. We shall see! Oh no, just a minute, you're not going
to stay here while I'm dreaming.

OLD BOY. Fine! I have no wish to be dreamt about by you.

OLD MAN. You expect *me* to dream about you? *Me?*

OLD BOY. And *you* think you're dreaming about me? *You?*

OLD MAN. Very well. I'll wake up. It was your idea.

OLD BOY (*less certainly*). I'm not afraid of you.

OLD MAN. You didn't want to leave my dream, voluntarily,
when I asked you to, so you'll leave it when I wake up. I'll
wake up and annihilate you. (*Closes his eyes and clenches his
fists.*)

OLD BOY (*frightened*). Oh my God!

OLD MAN. Wait! In one moment you'll disappear. (*Tenses himself
up terribly. Opens his eyes.*) Still here?

OLD BOY (*triumphantly*). Of course I am! Where did you think I'd be? (OLD MAN *closes his eyes and repeats the effort. Opens his eyes.*)

OLD MAN (*to himself*). He's still here.

OLD BOY. If you could see your face!

OLD MAN. I know! You're a nightmare!

OLD BOY. Do stop behaving like an idiot, old man.

THIRD PERSON (*winding her hair into a knot*). My God! What a bore he is ...

OLD MAN AND OLD BOY (*together*). Who? (THIRD PERSON *shrugs her shoulders. Both men walk towards her.*)

OLD BOY. I've got an idea. We'll ask her which of us is dreaming about her.

OLD MAN (*enthusiastically*). Fine! (*Less enthusiastically.*) But if she says it's you, remember, I was against the idea.

OLD BOY (*stepping forward*). Excuse me, madam ... (*Waves his hand and hesitates.*) No, it's no good.

OLD MAN. Why not? You started off fine.

OLD BOY. If I'm dreaming about her and you together, it means that in her mind I don't exist and that she doesn't know a thing about me. In that case the only other person who exists in her mind is you, and later it might perhaps occur to her that you are dreaming about her. On the other hand, if you are dreaming about her and me, I'm the only person who exists in her mind. So whether she says I'm dreaming about her or you're dreaming about her, her answer will have no significance whatsoever.

OLD MAN. Why not? If she says you're dreaming about her, it means really I'm dreaming about her, and vice versa.

OLD BOY. Only on the surface. Because how can we be certain that two people who are being dreamt about exist for each other directly, and not simply through the agency of the person who's dreaming?

OLD MAN. Anyway, I know you're not dreaming about me. I can see you.

OLD BOY. I can see you, too.

OLD MAN. A fine state of affairs. What are we going to do?

OLD BOY. There is one possibility left: we're dreaming about each other.

OLD MAN. You about me and me ... about you?

OLD BOY. That's right. Mutually and simultaneously.

OLD MAN. And what about her?

OLD BOY. Unfortunately, it means both of us are dreaming about her.

OLD MAN. What rotten luck! The whole world dreams separately, and we're the only ones ...

OLD BOY. However, if we accept that we are dreaming about each other mutually and simultaneously, it means ...

OLD MAN. Why don't I ever dream like this at home?

OLD BOY. It means ... Oh, yes, there's more to it than this.

OLD MAN. What? Haven't we got enough troubles?

OLD BOY. Listen, old man: has it occurred to you that you're dreaming about me, and I'm dreaming about you, and we're both dreaming mutually on some unknown previous occasion?

OLD MAN. Now what on earth is that supposed to mean?

OLD BOY (*with growing excitement*). Neither of us knows how frequent this recurring cycle of dreams is. Let me explain: let us assume, say, that I am dreaming, for example, about you. And you, this person I am dreaming about, may, in turn, dream about me. And in this case I am no longer myself, but you, being dreamed about by me. And then I, in my turn, can dream about you and so on. And all this is happening externally and in depth, and in addition simultaneous and equilibrious with you.

OLD MAN. What's wrong with that?

OLD BOY. What's wrong? I should simply like to know whether a man who is being dreamt about by someone whom he was dreaming about previously when he was simultaneously being dreamt about by that man, can exist at all.

OLD MAN. So what you mean to say is that ... that we don't exist at all.

OLD BOY (*sits down exhausted and depressed*). Very possibly.

OLD MAN. ... and that we aren't here.

OLD BOY. No. We *are* here, but we don't exist.

OLD MAN. My God! What happens now?

OLD BOY. I don't know.

OLD MAN. You don't know?! You worked all this out with your beautiful scientific intellect, and now you say you don't know.

OLD BOY. Now then, old man, don't lose your temper.

OLD MAN. Don't lose my temper! When I'm suddenly told I'm not here!

OLD BOY. You are here. It's just that you don't exist.

OLD MAN. It's the same thing! You can't live if you don't exist!

OLD BOY. I'm afraid I can't answer that one.

OLD MAN. But I've got my passport, I've got my identity card! I'll show you, I'll prove my identity! I'll show you who I am. (*Forgetting that he is wearing pyjamas, he makes as if to rummage in his pockets and find his identity card.*)

OLD BOY. Your identity card doesn't mean a thing. I'm dreaming about you and your identity card (*to himself*) and you're doing the same.

OLD MAN. So we aren't *us* at all?

OLD BOY. That's right.

OLD MAN. And who is us?

OLD BOY. I told you, I don't know.

OLD MAN (*clenching his fists*). E-e-e, just wait till I meet the one that's me. I'll show him! (*Breaking down and crying.*) Who am I, old boy, who am I?

OLD BOY. I don't know, I just don't know.

OLD MAN. I must be someone! (*Shouts, walking about the stage.*) Who am I? Who am I?

OLD BOY. Shhh! Be quiet!

OLD MAN. What do you mean? Why should I be quiet? And what about you, eh, do you know who you are?

OLD BOY (*with the first signs of alarm*). No. But I'm going to find out.

OLD MAN. How are you going to find out? Who from?

OLD BOY (*standing up, threateningly*). What's it got to do with you?

OLD MAN (*struck by the unnaturalness of his voice, appearance and demeanour*). I'm asking out ... out of curiosity.

OLD BOY (*shouting*). I must exist! I must!

OLD MAN (*startled, putting his hand on the other's shoulder*). Now then, old boy, calm down. You're you. That's all right, isn't it? Let's forget all about it. Chin up! The dawn will come and if you don't exist today you'll exist tomorrow. Anyway here we are together on a delegation, don't you remember? You remember the old office, don't you? And the boss, eh? ... What are you doing?

OLD BOY (*falls down on his knees in front of* THIRD PERSON). Forgive me! I have resisted too long! For years I have waited for you! Through you I shall be, I shall exist! Around me it's everything, it's always, it's everywhere, and I – where am I? Tell me!

OLD MAN. Please, old boy, control yourself ...

OLD BOY. Save me from the universe which is nothingness.

OLD MAN. Look, old boy, will you try and control yourself. For my sake, old boy, stop this, please.

OLD BOY. Help me! Let me *be*! Just me, just here, just now! (*Takes* THIRD PERSON *by the hand.*) Swear to me!

THIRD PERSON. Leave me alone.

OLD BOY. Grant me salvation!

   (THIRD PERSON *has hitherto been listening to* OLD BOY's *tirade with care, but at the same time looking closely around her. She does not allow her hand to be taken, but gets up and puts on her shoes. Her reply to* OLD BOY *takes the form of one word uttered in a tone of surprise, though this surprise is related not so much to* OLD BOY's *suggestion as to the word itself.*)

THIRD PERSON. Salvation?

OLD BOY. And let me be neither as a sounding brass nor as a tinkling cymbal, but simply me.

OLD MAN. He's gone mad.

   (THIRD PERSON *lifts the candlestick from the table.*)

OLD BOY. Where are you going? (THIRD PERSON *blows at the flames of the candles and extinguishes them. Complete darkness.*) Don't go away! Stay here! (*Running feet, sounds of a struggle.*) I won't let you go! (*Inarticulate sounds.*) Ah, I have you! You're mine! Mine!

(His cries are gradually drowned by the approach of a train, and then by the usual sharp whistle. Noise of the train going away. Another frightful whistle, though a bit quieter. The light of the standard lamp is turned on. OLD BOY is lying across the bed nearest the door, embracing OLD MAN who has just a moment ago managed to reach the switch of the standard lamp. The candlestick is standing on the table as before.)

OLD BOY. Eerr, oh! It's you ...

OLD MAN. Yyyes ...

OLD BOY *(transferring himself to his own bed, the one with the bad spring)*. I'm terribly sorry.

OLD MAN. Did you want something, old boy?

OLD BOY. No, no ... I just ... You must excuse me.

OLD MAN. It doesn't matter in the slightest, not the slightest ... You know something?

OLD BOY. What, old man?

OLD MAN. If they don't give us single rooms tomorrow night, I'm going to sleep at the station.

OLD BOY. I really must apologize, old man.

OLD MAN. I tell you, it doesn't matter. *(Pause. Both men lie on their backs, staring up at the ceiling.)* ... Er, old boy?

OLD BOY. Yes, old man.

OLD MAN. ... are you asleep?

OLD BOY. Not yet.

OLD MAN. Tell me, old boy, were you dreaming just then? *(Pause)*.

OLD BOY. No. *(Pause.)* ... What about you? *(Pause.)*

OLD MAN. No, I wasn't either.

OLD BOY *(with relief)*. Well, good night, then.

OLD MAN *(with relief)*. Good night! *(Turns the light off.)*